BEDSIDE BOOK OF

CRICKET CENTURIES

BEDSIDE BOOK OF
CRICKET CENTURIES

TERRY SMITH

ANGUS & ROBERTSON
An imprint of HarperCollins*Publishers*

ANGUS & ROBERTSON
An imprint of HarperCollinsPublishers

First published in Australia in 1991 by
CollinsAngus&Robertson Publishers Pty Limited (ACN 009 913 517)
A division of HarperCollinsPublishers (Australia) Pty Limited
Unit 4, Eden Park Estate, 31 Waterloo Road, North Ryde
NSW 2113, Australia

HarperCollinsPublishers (New Lealand) Limited
31 View Road, Glenfield, Auckland 10, New Zealand

HarperCollinsPublishers Limited
77–85 Fulham Palace Road, London W6 8JB, United Kingdom

National Library of Australia
Cataloguing-in-Publication data:
Smith, Terry, 1937— .
Bedside book of cricket centuries.
Includes index.
ISBN 0 207 17066 5.
1. Cricket players — Interviews. 2. Cricket — Records.
I. Title.
796.358092

Cover photograph: David Davies AP
Sporting Pix
Printed in Australia by Griffin Press

5 4 3 2 1
95 94 93 92 91

CONTENTS

ACKNOWLEDGEMENTS

Thanks go to the authors for permission to quote from *The Barry Richards Story*, by Barry Richards (Angus & Robertson Publishers 1978) and *One for the Road*, by Doug Walters (Swan Publishing 1988).

Other books and publications consulted in confirming facts were *Game of a Lifetime*, by Denzil Batchelor (Werner Laurie 1953); *Fingleton on Cricket*, by Jack Fingleton (Collins 1972); *On Top Down Under*, by Ray Robinson (Cassell 1975); *Border — An Autobiography*, by Allan Border (Methuen 1986); *Diary of the Ashes*, by Geoff Lawson (Angus & Robertson Publishers 1988); *Denis Compton's Test Diary* (Adlard and Son 1964); *Wisden's Cricketers Almanack* (Sporting Handbooks and MacDonald Jane); *Cricket Beyond the Bazaar*, by Mike Coward (Allen and Unwin 1990); *Great Innings*, by Peter Roebuck (Pan Books 1990).

FOREWORD

This is not a cricket book that will cause *Wisden's Cricketers Almanack* to be burned at the Sydney Cricket Ground. Unlike some of the human rottweilers of the cricket-writing world, I'm a humble scribbler. I simply approached some of the world's finest batsmen and enquired what was their finest century. From Keith Miller and Neil Harvey to current heroes Allan Border, Dean Jones, Steve and Mark Waugh and Graeme Hick, they unhesitatingly gave of their time.

Unlike other books of centuries by much more knowledgeable cricket writers, this volume simply sets the scene and lets the player himself (or herself) tell the story. A few had an amazingly vivid memory of events, while others, particularly my own special hero Keith Miller, needed prodding into action.

Recalling how he revelled in an all-night party with South African golfer Bobby Locke in Brisbane on the eve of a NSW v Queensland game, Keith said cheerfully: 'Bobby won the Australian Open the next day and I went to the Gabba, had a snooze and went out and pottered about for a while. Just managed to hang in there.' The scorecard for that day reads – K. Miller, bowled R. Archer 164.

There were a few surprises. For instance, Bill Lawry bypassed his epic 130 at Lord's in 1961 when balls were whizzing like Scud missiles off a ridge in the pitch, to choose an innings in a Melbourne grade final as his most satisfying performance. Putting his long-awaited first Test century on the back burner, Steve Waugh plumped for the 100 he hit for Somerset in his first taste of the atom-splitting, rocket-propelled balls of a West Indian Test fast bowler.

According to David Hookes, he was confronted mid-pitch by a snarling Tony Greig after he had carved five successive fours from the English skipper in the 1977 Centenary Test in Melbourne. 'Why don't you piss off?' demanded Greig in his clipped South African accent.

Hookes shot back: 'Better an Australian playing for Australia than a f------ Pommy import.'

When wicketkeeper Rod Marsh scored his finest century in this game, he carried in his hip pocket a picture of Jack Blackham, who had been Australia's gloveman in the very first Test against England 100 years earlier.

Allan Border told of the bowler who made him feel totally out of his depth in Test cricket, while Dean Jones vividly recalled the century in

India which almost killed him. I got the feeling Norm O'Neill would like to strangle the idiot who first pinned the tag of 'the new Don Bradman' to his reluctant chest. Still, he scored six picket-peppering Test centuries which were a joy to watch.

Denise Annetts and Lindsay Reeler proved pleasing ambassadors for women's cricket, so often neglected in books on the sport.

While whipping up a world record 193 run out against England in 1987, Denise Annetts figured in a world record partnership of 309 with Lindsay Reeler. A year later, Lindsay's stylish strokes gave her a stunning average of 149.33 per innings in spite of a duck when Australia won the World Cup in Melbourne.

I was so hoping to chat with Sir Donald Bradman, whose genius made cricket's record books almost burst their bindings, but the great man politely turned down my request. I didn't feel too badly about it as he has given only a handful of interviews in the last 40 years. In the autumn of his life, he prefers to stay in the shadows.

So what I hope is a snug bedside book — by a cricket nut for fellow cricket nuts — is sadly incomplete, but at least I tried.

Of course, the Don long ago went on record to say that his blue-ribbon 254 against England in the Lord's Test in 1930 was his greatest-ever knock. With Australia chasing 425, he walked to the wicket and butchered the English bowlers with the wrists of a fencer and the foot-work of a dancing master.

Bradman recalled: 'That innings was the nearest to technical perfection. Apart from one or two exceptions, every ball went where I intended it to go. I never hit the ball anywhere but in the middle of the bat and I never lifted one off the ground until the stroke from which I was out to the best catch I ever saw.'

Still, I once got Sir Donald's copperplate autograph and as a kid I sat awestruck while he hit his 100th century against India one Saturday afternoon in 1947 at the Sydney Cricket Ground.

Those were the days when tennis star Fred Stolle and I wrestled with pulleys, numbers and nameplates in the Waitara Oval scoreboard each Saturday while a rookie called Alan Davidson lifted the Northern District side to premiership honours with his six-hitting and devilish left-arm bowling.

I've got such a lot of people to thank for their help and encouragement on this book. Firstly, the centurions themselves. It was a pleasure to drink, gossip and laugh with them. Gratitude to Kim Anderson, my charming publisher; Ross Dunbar and Stephen Gibbs, those walking encyclopedias of cricket who run the NSW Cricket Association's remarkable library; my employers at News Limited; and my old friend Frank Misson, once a lion-hearted fast bowler for Australia, who opened so many doors.

And especially Sybilla.

Terry Smith, 1991

KEITH MILLER

With his six-hitting and fast bowling, Keith Miller was the hero of a generation of Australian kids.

KEITH MILLER

So hale and hearty and full of beans in his seventies, Keith Miller, one of the great all-rounders of all time and probably the most glamorous figure to play for Australia at anything, confesses to a lifelong love affair with Lord's.

Lord's is a worldly, knowing sort of place set in St John's Wood in the heart of London. It has the coolness of the old school tie coupled with a raciness and a sophistication that sets it above all other cricket grounds.

'The atmosphere grabs you,' Miller says in his warm, cheerful gravel voice. 'I'm a bit of a romantic, and you'd walk down those two little steps onto the ground and you'd think, jeez, these are the same two steps W.G. Grace and Victor Trumper walked down.

'I didn't like it at first, but I got to love the place. I always did well at Lord's too. I ground it out for 100 there against England in 1953 and took wickets at Lord's in the 1956 Test. That's all I remember. You'll have to look it up in the records.'

Only Keith Miller, scorer of almost 3000 Test runs (including seven centuries and 30 huge, meaty Test sixes) and taker of 170 Test wickets with his volatile fast bowling, could so shrug off his majestic deeds at Lord's in 1956.

Beset with back problems in his 37th year, Miller bowled 70 overs to take five wickets in each innings and contributed 58 runs to hoist Australia to a 1–0 series lead. As the Australians left the field, he pinched a bail from an umpire's pocket and tossed it in a grand gesture to some youngsters in the crowd.

That was the style of Keith Ross Miller (born 28 November 1919 in Melbourne), the definitive sporting legend — Test cricketer, State footballer for Victoria, dashing film star looks with a thick, swept-back mane of black hair, night fighter pilot, and no stranger to bookies. He was larger than life and saw cricket as something much less than trench warfare.

If he was batting or bowling, this Mosquito Bomber pilot in World War Two was one of the great bar emptiers of all time. That was the magic of Miller. He'd suddenly toss back his hair and change the course of a whole match in a handful of overs. And if he wasn't batting, bowling or watching the dressing room for a signal that he'd backed a winner, Miller would swoop like a seagull to grab a blinding slips catch.

If you ignore the fact that he had an artificial hip inserted when he was

66, Miller gives the impression he could still shrug off a hangover and take the new ball at the Sydney Cricket Ground without too much difficulty. Or at least he'd give it a go.

In the midst of Australia's bicentennial celebrations, a group of Marylebone Cricket Club bigwigs from Lord's were invited to the Sydney Town Hall for cocktails while a Test match was being played at the SCG. Miller was chatting with Colonel John Stephenson, the MCC secretary, when up strutted a man wearing one of those hideous orange and yellow striped MCC ties.

'Colonel Stephenson?' he demanded.

'That's right.'

'I've just heard you're the boss at Lord's.'

Pointing to Miller, Colonel Stephenson said: 'No, I'm not, this chap is.'

'Well, I am a life member at Lord's,' said Miller as he recalled the incident with obvious relish. 'Now I walk in as if I own the place.'

So it's hardly surprising Miller nominates his epic 185 with seven sixes for a Dominions XI against England at Lord's in 1945 just after the Second World War as the innings he cherishes above all. Now living in retirement in the idyllic Sydney beachside suburb of Newport, where he takes it easy, having the odd beer and a bet between stints of gardening, Miller recalls:

> I hit a couple of sixes into the old stand. It was my best innings ever. Even Jim Swanton [the legendary English critic] said Lord's wasn't big enough to hold me. Walter Hammond got a couple of centuries in that game and Learie Constantine, the great West Indian player, was in the Dominions team.
>
> Those Victory Tests we had just after the war was the best cricket I ever played. It was great stuff. The matter of life and death was behind us and after six years we were back to normal. Cricket was a game and not a war.
>
> The result didn't mean anything more than a pat on the back for the winner and a drink together in the bar. What a pity it is that cricket isn't played like that today. The importance attached to winning and losing has become hopelessly distorted.

Miller's memory can be a trifle hazy over such things, so I quote from the purple prose of Denzil Batchelor, the noted English writer:

> On the Tuesday morning, the mood of the Dominions soon declared itself. Miller sprang at the bowling and shook the life out of it. He released all his pent-up aggression at Hollies and twice in an over he hit soaring sixes off booming straight drives. His score had stood at 61 when stumps were drawn

on the previous night. Within 90 minutes he had raised it to 185. After Donnelly had been yorked by Wright, Constantine arrived to help Miller cram on the pace. It was a schoolboy's dream.

The two men went for the bowling not only with Rabelaisian appetites, but also with Rabelaisian wit. Hammond was forced to set a field for Jack Davies which contained no slip or gully; indeed, the nearest fieldsman seemed to be in Mesopotamia, while the farther bodies were pretty well astral.

With the game slipping from underfoot in flashing landslide, I should have decided to give the ball to James Langridge. So, too, did Hammond decide. If anyone could call the game to order, it must be that experienced, hard-working master of his craft. Surely no one would dare subject solid James Langridge to the sort of treatment that had been going the rounds? It would be like asking Sir Alfred Munnings to participate in some surrealist romp.

Well, James Langridge's first over yielded three stratospheric sixes; two from Miller, shaking his bronzed mane from his gleaming eyes. In three-quarters of an hour he and Constantine had added 117 between them: and this against pretty well the best bowling in England.

Before cracking Wright's faster ball into Langridge's palms at cover, Miller had hit seven sixes in his third century in four matches at Lord's during the summer. The biggest of them will be talked of almost as long as Albert Trott's classic stroke. It came off an inoffensive, indeed, well-behaved ball from Hollies — which found itself whirled away to seek shelter on the roof of the broadcasting hut above the England dressing room.

This was the innings which provoked The Times' correspondent to admit that he had never seen hitting like this in 60 years' experience at Lord's.

Miller recalls:

During the war, I used to play a lot of one-day matches at Lord's on Saturday afternoons. RAF v RAAF or Army or Fire Brigade. Whatever you liked. In those wartime games, they'd let people sit on the grass and they'd have 35,000 at a ground that normally holds about 24,000. So I got used to playing there.

A lot of my old mates were killed in a raid on Bournemouth on a day I was called away to play in a match at Lord's. I would have been with them but for that.

Lord's and the Sydney Cricket Ground. I loved them and always did well there. Before they built all the stands, the Sydney ground was magnificent. The Hill, a beautiful surface, the green turreted pavilions, plenty of breeze. Now the stands block all the air out. I've always said the best ground for atmosphere is Lord's and the best playing conditions are in Sydney. If some smart alec chips me about this, I say if Don Bradman and I agree on something, it's got to be right. Old Don and I differed on cricket tactics at times, usually when I was bowling.

Miller and Bradman were always seen as incompatible figures; there are many legends of bad blood between them. In fact, Bradman invariably gets the blame for Miller not getting the Australian captaincy he so richly deserved. Miller was, in the administrative eye, intolerably extrovert; he was thought to have hurled one or two bouncers and epithets towards the wrong target. When Miller was omitted from the Australian team to tour South Africa in 1949–50, despite being unarguably the world's number one all-rounder, Jack Fingleton accused Bradman of waging a vendetta against Miller. Happily, Miller joined the tour as a replacement player and, typically, took the series by the throat.

Miller comments:

It is quite true Bradman and I had a couple of disagreements during Test matches. One was at Lord's when I lobbed the ball back at him when he tried to get me to bowl. My back is a finicky bloody thing, like the Melbourne weather. When I woke up on the second day of that Lord's Test in 1948, I couldn't move. My back was stuffed and I told Don in the dressing room that I had no hope of bowling. I'd love to have taken the new ball because the wicket was a greentop, the best in the world for a pace bowler.

Ray Lindwall bowled one over and I'm walking to the other end when Don stopped me. 'Nugget,' he said, 'will you try one over?' I'd already told him my back was crook, so when Don handed me the ball, I dollied it back to him. He'd made a monkey out of me in the middle of Lord's but I suppose he was just trying to pressurise me.

'Grind them into the dust,' Don would say when we were playing the Poms. I thought, bugger me, we've just finished a war and everyone is happy to be alive and now we have to grind them into the dust. Still, in spite of our few tiffs, I have always admired Don enormously.

They loved Miller in England, where he wrote for the *Daily Express* and would turn up at Ascot wearing top hat and tails. The Errol Flynn of cricket, they called him. It made the front pages in 1956 when he finished a day's cricket and was whisked by Rolls Royce to dine with Princess Margaret at Lord Mountbatten's stately home, Broadlands.

Famed for his love of horse racing, Miller still makes an annual pilgrimage to the Melbourne Cup. He was so close to champion jockey Scobie Breasley that when he went to the races in England, he would be approached by lords and cockney touts for tips. On one occasion the

Duke of Norfolk asked: 'Tell me, Keith. Which one of my horses does Scobie think he can win on today?' He claims the biggest disappointment of his childhood was when he learned he was too big to become an apprentice jockey.

From royalty down, men and women have been entranced by this dashing, debonair, defiant man who was adored by the crowds during his 55 Tests. On Christmas Day 1990, John Major, Britain's new Prime Minister, rang unexpectedly just to wish him a Merry Christmas. Yet Miller is just as happy having lunch in Sydney's Chinatown with a group of garbos as dining at the venerable East India club in London.

Prime Minister Sir Robert Menzies was such an admirer that he kept a classic action shot of Miller's upright square cut on the wall of his office in Parliament House. He wrote in his memoirs: 'The feet are beautifully placed, the lithe body balanced and yet leaning out of balance with the shot; the blade through over the left shoulder, the head triumphant, the eye looking toward the boundary. It is a beautiful piece of sculpture and would have provoked immense joy in ancient Athens.'

Miller unashamedly played up to the crowd at times because he felt he was there to give them entertainment. With the new ball in his hand he produced the unexpected. He might bowl a quickish leg break, then take a short run and fire down the most ferocious bouncer.

After the big fellow had destroyed the 1951–52 West Indian tourists who included the immortal trio of Frank Worrell, Everton Weekes and Clyde Walcott, skipper John Goodard declared: 'Give us Keith Miller and we'll beat the world.'

With England needing a mere 92 to win the 1955 Adelaide Test and secure the Ashes, vice-captain Miller was asked who would win. 'I haven't a clue,' he said with a challenging glint in his eye, 'but somebody's in for a nasty half-hour.' In 20 balls, Miller fired out Bill Edrich, Len Hutton and Colin Cowdrey. Then he hurled himself under a low drive by Peter May to take a staggeringly difficult catch at extra cover. 4 for 49. But Miller's shoulder was injured making the catch, and Australia's vision of victory was gone.

Then there was the famous day in the 1955–56 season when Miller took 7 for 12 off 7.3 overs (five clean-bowled) to whip out South Australia for 27, still a record low total in a Sheffield Shield game. He recalls:

> I was captain of the State side and I'd closed the innings just before stumps. That night my youngest boy Bobby was born, so we drank a lot of grog to celebrate. I was pretty crook the next morning, I can tell you.
>
> I was supposed to pick up Peter Philpott, who lived near me, but I bloody

forgot until I got to the Harbour Bridge. I had to double back 15 miles and by the time we got to the ground the umpires were going out. I was still doing up my shoes as we went out.

I had a few balls left from an unfinished over, and I felt so horrible I said to Alan Davidson, 'Davo, I'm not feeling too good. I'll finish this over and you take over.' Next thing — bing, bing, bing — 7 for 12. I could see six stumps at the other end, so how could I miss them?'

Another famous hangover story occurred during a Shield game against Queensland in Brisbane which coincided with South African golfer Bobby Locke playing in the 1955 Australian Open there. Over to Miller: 'Ray Lindwall and I knew Bobby from South Africa. What a character. We had a party in his hotel room and next morning we could hardly lift our heads. Bobby won the Australian Open that day and I went to the Gabba, had a snooze in the dressing room and went out and pottered about for a while. Just managed to hang in there.'

Pottered about? The scorebook for that day reads – Miller, bowled Ron Archer 164.

Like a grenade with a loose pin liable to explode when you least expect it, Miller once hit the first ball of a Test day's play out of the Adelaide Oval. He recalls:

I hit a lot of big sixes. When I was playing for Victoria, I hit Arthur Morris onto the roof of the Members' Stand at the Sydney Cricket Ground. I got another big one in Sydney off Alec Bedser, the English bowler, which hit the wall at the back of the old Sheridan Stand. Bedser was medium-fast, and I hit some of my really big ones off the medium pacers. At that speed, the ball really ricochets off the bat. People ask if I made up my mind to go for a six before the ball was bowled. Off the slow bowlers I've done this plenty of times, but it's not on against a fast bowler. You'd look a nice goose if you set yourself for a hook and the ball was up in the blockhole.

Relishing a medium-paced ball from Victoria's Sam Loxton, Miller hammered it into the top deck of the M.A. Noble stand, one of the biggest hits ever seen at the Sydney Cricket Ground. But he believes the three huge sixes he struck from NSW's Ernie Toshack at the Melbourne Cricket Ground in 1946 travelled just as far.

Miller didn't give a hoot for averages and relished the chance to help a colleague achieve glory. When Bradman scored his 100th century for an Australian XI against India at the SCG in 1947, Miller unashamedly took a back seat and became little more than the great man's running partner. When he became captain of NSW in 1953, he'd often spin a coin to pick who'd go in at five, six, seven and eight. That kept everybody happy and interested. Neil Harvey was quick to pay credit to Miller for his Test century against England at Leeds in 1948, scored when only 19 years old. Speaking at Keith's 70th birthday gathering, Harvey said:

> I didn't get it. Keith Miller got it for me. When my turn came to bat, we'd lost three quick wickets [Morris, Hassett, Bradman]. I went out and Keith told me to go down to the bowler's end and have a look at Jim Laker for a while. He said he'd take the strike.
>
> Next over Keith slammed Laker back over his head for six and then repeated it soon after. He walked down the wicket and asked, 'Feel better?' Those two shots and his comradeship paved the way for my 100.

Bewitched by Miller's classic innings of 58, Denzil Batchelor wrote:

> For an hour and a half, Miller went his bandit's way, continuing to ravage and despoil. His driving had all the heady beauty of flamboyance. He was the rider of whirlwinds; and here was his chance. Pollard tore into him, the length well disciplined, each ball spurred into thrilling speed off the pitch. Miller flung back his lion's mane, and drove his heart and soul into a follow-through that might have come out of some masterpiece among the Elgin Marbles.

John Warr, the England cricketer who later became president of the MCC, described Miller as a Cavalier in a world of Roundheads. Everything he did, from throwing the ball back to Bradman after declining the captain's command to bowl at Lord's to turning up to net practice in a dinner suit on his way home from a party, was without precedent.

One cannot help but wonder what havoc Miller would have created in one-day cricket with his six-hitting, devastating fast bowling and glorious fielding. However, the great man isn't too impressed with this facet of the game. 'It's all bullshit,' he says. 'I liken it to television wrestling and that roller game thing. You see great players play a couple of good shots and then make a swish you'd kick a ten-year-old kid up the arse for doing. The great brilliance of these batsmen has been lost.'

Typically, Miller nominates the Rev James Aitchison, a Scottish clergyman, and Walter Hadlee, father of Richard, as scoring two of the greatest centuries he has ever seen. He says:

> I include the Bradmans, Huttons and Harveys when I say the Rev Aitchison hit one of the best centuries I've ever seen. Ray Lindwall and I were playing in

> this game against Scotland in Glasgow and he hammered us. It was a miserable day; bloody awful, yet he whipped up 100 out of 170-odd. I rank that above a lot of centuries.
>
> Walter Hadlee got 190-odd against Australia in Dunedin in 1946. Lindwall was playing, too. Hadlee wore glasses and there was a fair bit of rain, but he played a terrific innings. They're the ones I remember.

Of course, Miller professed to remember more about those innings than his own drama-charged efforts which thrilled the cricket world. That's why this modest champion was everybody's cricket hero.

There are so many sides to Keith Miller. A lover of classical music, he once detoured on a flight across the Rhineland to take a look at Bonn, where Beethoven was born. It was on a wartime stopover in Boston on the way from Australia to England that he met his wife Peg, whom he wed in 1946 and who has seen him play cricket only three or four times. Golf is another passion, but sadly Keith's plastic hip has forced him to give up the game. 'I'd be too wobbly out on the course,' he says.

Perhaps it's because Miller was my schoolboy hero, but as far as I'm concerned only Sir Gary Sobers would be a match for him in today's one-day games. If Keith was playing now, he would be constantly in the headlines, but never for indulging in the yobbo antics of Ian Botham and Co. Although a swashbuckler, old Nugget had far too much style for that.

THE DOMINIONS v ENGLAND
Lords, 25–28 August 1945

The Dominions

D.R. Fell c Griffith b Wright	12	b Davies	28
H.S. Craig c Davies b Phillipson	56	c Hammond b Davies	32
J. Pettiford b Davies	1	b Wright	6
K.R. Miller lbw b Hollies	26	c Langridge b Wright	185
M.P. Donnelly c and b Hollies	133	b Wright	29
L.N. Constantine c Hollies b Wright	5	c Fishlock b Hollies	40
C.G. Pepper c Hammond b Wright	51	c Robertson b Hollies	1
D.R. Cristofani lbw b Edrich	6	b Wright	5
R.G. Williams lbw b Wright	11	c Hammond b Wright	0
R.S. Ellis b Wright	0	st Griffith b Hollies	0
C.D. Bremner not out	1	not out	0
Sundries	5		10
	307		336

	O	M	R	W	O	M	R	W
Phillipson	16	2	40	1	2	1	1	0
Edrich	9	1	19	1	3	0	13	0
Wright	30	2	90	5	30.1	6	105	5
Davies	22	9	43	1	13	3	35	2
Hollies	20.2	3	86	2	29	8	115	3
Langridge	6	1	24	0	8	0	57	0

England

L.B. Fishlock c Pettiford b Ellis	12	run out	7
J.D. Robertson lbw b Constantine	4	c Fell b Pettiford	5
J. Langridge lbw b Cristofani	28	b Pepper	15
W.E. Phillipson b Pepper	0	run out	14
S.G. Griffith c Bremner b Williams	15	c Pepper b Pettisford	36
W.R. Hammond st Bremner b Pepper	121	st Bremner c Cristofani	102
H. Gimblett c Pettiford b Cristofani	11	b Pepper	30
W.J. Edrich c Pepper b Cristofani	78	c Pepper b Ellis	31
J.G.W. Davies lbw p Pepper	1	b Pepper	56
D.V.P. Wright lbw b Pepper	0	b Cristofani	0
E. Hollies not out	0	not out	15
Sundries	17		15
	287		311

	O	M	R	W	O	M	R	W
Miller	1	0	2	0	5	0	28	0
Williams	22	4	49	1	2	0	11	0
Constantine	15	2	53	1	6	0	27	0
Pepper	18	3	57	4	33	13	67	3
Ellis	4	3	4	1	20	4	54	1
Cristofani	23.3	4	82	3	21.3	1	64	2
Pettiford	5	0	23	0	14	3	45	2

The Dominions won by 45 runs

NEIL HARVEY

When it came to charm and nimble footwork, no Australian batsman could match Neil Harvey, who hit a Test century against England when he was 19 years old.

NEIL HARVEY

'It is not strength, but art, obtains the prize.' Homer, *The Iliad*

The skip to the pitch of the ball, the swing of the bat — and there was another Neil Harvey shot racing to the boundary. When it came to charm and nimble footwork, no Australian batsman could match him.

For 15 years Harvey was the darling of the cricket world as he plundered 21 Test centuries from some of the world's best bowlers at an average of 48.4, starting with 112 in his first Test against England in 1948 when he was only 19 years old.

He was never, never dull to watch as he got his 6149 Test runs from the fireballs of Frank Tyson, Wes Hall and Freddie Trueman, the cut and swing of Alec Bedser, Fazal Mahmood and Gary Sobers and the spin of Jim Laker, Tony Lock, Sonny Ramadhin, Alf Valentine and Hugh Tayfield.

Invariably capless, Harvey would travel so far down the pitch to collar the spinners that one declared: 'He kept coming so far along the track towards me that I thought he must want to shake my hand.' Yet not one stumping figures among his 127 dismissals in 79 Tests.

Although a vote of his peers would have given him the Australian captaincy ahead of Ian Craig in the 1950s, there was much delight when Harvey led Australia to a thrilling victory in the 1961 Lord's Test against England when Richie Benaud was injured. Sadly, this was the only Test team he ever captained.

Born on 3 October 1928 in Fitzroy, Melbourne, Robert Neil Harvey learned to play cricket with his five brothers using a kerosene tin wicket and a tennis ball on cobblestones. Three of his brothers — Mervyn, Clarrie and Ray — made Sheffield Shield centuries, with Mervyn playing a single Test as an opener against England in 1946–47.

In spite of being a magnificent cover fieldsman before becoming a brilliant slips catcher who snared a record-equalling six catches against England in his farewell Test in 1963, Harvey's reputation for kestrel eyesight was blown during tests by a Johannesburg optometrist in 1957. On discovering Neil was surprisingly short-sighted, he asked: 'Who leads you out to bat?'

Harvey explains: 'I knew I was a bit on the short-sighted side. I could see the ball alright when I batted, but often wondered why I couldn't read the scoreboard from the middle of the ground.'

With Australia needing quick runs against South Africa in the 1953

Adelaide Test, Harvey whipped up a chanceless century in only 106 minutes, the fastest Test 100 in Australia since the war. Fittingly, he was made a Member of the British Empire for services to cricket.

When asking Harvey to choose his finest century, I thought he would have plumped for the second of his 21 Test 100s — 112 against England at Leeds when a tyro of 19. But no, the great man gives pride of place to his 151 not out against South Africa on a brute of a wicket at Durban in 1950. It occurred after a virtual game of poker in which Australia's Lindsay Hassett outbluffed rival skipper Dudley Nourse by not trying to bowl the South Africans out. Harvey recalls:

> We lost the toss and South Africa finished the first day at 2 for 240. There was a thunderstorm that night which made the wicket like a Brisbane sticky, so we were in no hurry to get caught on it. The guys were told to bowl just outside the stumps without any turn on the ball and try to keep down runs without taking wickets. Bill Johnston, in particular, was superb in this role.
>
> After they'd got to 311, we were shot out for 75 in two hours, with their off spinner Hugh Tayfield taking 7 for 23. Lindsay Hassett put me at number nine in case we could bat out the day, but we couldn't last the distance.
>
> On Monday morning Dudley Nourse, the South African captain, got a weather bureau forecast saying there would be another storm that night. Rather than make us follow on, he decided to bat again and if the rain did indeed come, he'd get us on another sticky. If he'd put us in again, they'd have killed us. There was no way we could have got out of it.
>
> South Africa were out for 99, with Bill Johnston (bowling left-arm orthodox spinners) and Ian Johnson taking nine wickets between them. So we were left with 336 to win, and at stumps were 3 for 80 after losing Jack Moroney, Keith Miller and Lindsay Hassett. With the pitch playing the way it was, we gave ourselves no chance of winning.
>
> The wicket was pock-marked with holes all over it. We'd used the medium roller to try to get a bit of a hard top on it, and that did harden it up a little. Still, it was a real turner when Arthur Morris and I resumed on the last morning. The storm forecast had turned out to be a fizzer, but when Arthur went early to make us 4 for 95, our only thoughts were to try to bat out the day and save the match. There was no talk of winning. The spinners Tayfield and Tufty Mann, an orthodox left-armer, were turning it a couple of feet and you never knew if the ball was going to stand up or shoot after hitting one of the crumbling holes.
>
> Sam Loxton and I got together and the fifth wicket didn't fall until 230. Sam curbed his natural attacking instincts to play the innings of his life for 54. We

had to work for every run because Tayfield and Mann were very accurate. Eventually I reached my slowest-ever century.

If they bowled one a foot short, I'd go back and cut the ball through point. Otherwise I went down the wicket to them. I was reasonably good at that and most of my runs that day came from going down the pitch. With Tayfield and Mann bowling 101 overs between them and their fast bowler Cuan McCarthy getting only 12, there wasn't much variety in the South African attack.

At teatime we realised we had a good chance of winning, but when Sam got out there wasn't a lot left. However, Colin McCool played quite well and was there at the finish with 39. You get a lot of satisfaction out of winning a game by five wickets from a position like that.

The big thing about my 151 not out is that it came in the second innings on a dodgy pitch. Any batsman worth his salt should get runs in the first innings. When we toured the West Indies in 1955, I got a double 100 and a couple of single centuries in the Tests, but the wickets there were so good that took a lot of the gloss off it. Battling the elements as well as the bowling gave me much greater satisfaction than making 200 on a plumb track.

Thus the stage is set for Harvey's first Test against England at Leeds in 1948 in a scenario that could well have been contrived by a drama producer. Imagine: a tyro of 19 jauntily walks in to bat after the immortal Don Bradman's stumps have been shattered and Australia is in dire trouble at three for 68. Legend has it that Harvey walked up to Keith Miller and said: 'What's going on out here? Let's get stuck into them, eh?' Harvey recalls:

We were chasing 456 and I was due to bat at number five. There were no covers in those days, and the wicket was greasy from overnight rain. I went to put the pads on when Lindsay Hassett got out, and had time to put on only one pad when there was this tremendous roar as Dick Pollard sent Bradman's stumps flying. In the rush to get out onto the ground, I didn't have time to get nervous.

Having Keith Miller out there was a terrific help. He took me under his wing in the first half-hour and made a couple of tremendous hits for six from the off spinner Jim Laker. Twice in two overs I watched the ball sailing over my head for six, and I thought: 'Crikey, this isn't such a tough game after all.' Keith is such a great bloke as well. He talked to me a fair bit, but the big thing is that he showed me the way by example. That's what lifts your confidence.

Dishing out further punishment to Laker, Harvey made 112 off 183 balls, a stunning entry into the Test arena against England which prompted

Bill O'Reilly to say it was stamped with the hallmark of genius. He figured in a partnership of 121 with Miller before joining forces with bosom pal Sam Loxton in another century stand of 105.

Of course, some of Harvey's greatest innings didn't result in centuries, notably his 92 not out against Frank Tyson's thunderbolts in the second innings of the SCG Test on a greentop against England in 1954–55. He brackets Tyson with Wes Hall, of the West Indies, as the quickest bowlers he has seen, with Jeff Thomson, Charlie Griffith and Malcolm Marshall falling just short of this pair. Harvey is also proud of his back-to-the-wall innings of 70 and 69 at Leeds in 1956 when Jim Laker and Tony Lock were spinning the ball almost square on a dusty, sandy dirt wicket. On the Dacca mat, he made 96 against the deadly Fazal Mahmood while seven partners were falling for 48.

Harvey has fond memories of Australia's amazing victory at Old Trafford in 1961 when vice-captain to Richie Benaud, who captured 6 for 70 when Australia appeared to be in a hopeless position on the last day. He recalls:

> Ted Dexter was thrashing us all over the place when Richie went round the wicket to bowl his leg spinners into the rough. Then Dexter chased the leg break and got an edge to Wally Grout behind the stumps. I was at leg slip when Peter May, the England captain, came in next. Richie put one into the footmarks, Peter went to sweep and was bowled round his legs. May couldn't believe it and just stood there. I said, 'Sorry Peter. You're out.' We were more gentlemanly in those days.
>
> When England's last man, Brian Statham, came in, I had to almost wrestle the ball out of Richie's hand. He'd taken six wickets and wanted seven and was bowling well. Statham wasn't all that flash against pace, so I said, 'Piss off, Richie. You've done enough. Give it to Davo.' Alan Davidson promptly knocked Statham's middle stump out of the ground with his third ball and we'd won. Thank heavens he did.'

Harvey didn't miss a trick on a cricket field, and should have been Australian captain ahead of Ian Craig when Ian Johnson quit in 1957. However, Johnson is believed to have put in a report after the 1956 tour of England claiming neither Harvey nor Richie Benaud was real captaincy material. Utter nonsense, of course. In spite of being so badly done by, Harvey (as everybody knew he would) gave Craig and subsequently Benaud the staunchest possible support as their vice-captain.

In a chase for runs against the clock at Lahore, Harvey and right-hander Norm O'Neill realised the Pakistani's field-changing delays would deny them time to win. So left-handed Harvey allowed a ball to hit his wicket, enabling a right-handed pair to complete the chase and Australia to become the first visiting team to win a series in Pakistan.

Looking to the amazing tied Test against the West Indies in Brisbane in 1960, Harvey recalls:

> With three run outs in the last two overs, we were unlucky not to have won. Everyone thought the game was going to finish early, but Davo and Richie Benaud had an amazing partnership. Actually, if they'd cut the grass like Richie had asked, there would have been no tie. Wally Grout was run out going for a third run after the ball stopped a foot short of the fence. The groundsman left the mower in the shed because he thought the game would be over by lunchtime, and you know how the grass grows at the Gabba.

In his farewell game in first class cricket in 1963 at the age of 34, Harvey thrilled a Sydney crowd with his highest ever score of 231 not out for NSW against South Australia, carving 120 runs in the session between lunch and tea. His retirement was ridiculously premature, but he wanted to establish himself in the business world.

Appreciating his deep knowledge of the game, before Harvey turned 39 a Board of Control ballot made him an Australian selector with Sir Donald Bradman and Jack Ryder. Four years later he became chairman of selectors, prompting Harvey to comment later: 'I have suffered more abuse, more criticism and more everything than I ever did as a player. But being a selector was certainly a challenge.' During Harvey's tenure as chairman, Jeff Thomson was introduced as Dennis Lillee's new ball partner and Greg Chappell, Rod Marsh and Max Walker all got their big chance. In 1979 Harvey was sacked as selector amidst great controversy.

When Nelson Mandela was released from prison, after serving 27 years in jail for plotting the violent overthrow of the government, he announced he wanted to meet Harvey because he had taken an interest in the plight of the black majority in South Africa. 'It was a very difficult thing to do indeed,' Mandela said. 'He was brave enough to speak out for the black man.'

With 67 centuries and 21,699 first class runs at an average of 50.93, Neil Harvey was something special, unchallenged as our greatest left-hander even though Allan Border has scored more Test runs. As the late Ray Robinson so aptly put it: 'Had Michelangelo been a cricketer, he would have batted like Harvey, with the touch that made chips of marble fly everywhere as he pressed on with the creation of a great piece of sculpture.'

AUSTRALIA v SOUTH AFRICA
Durban, 20–24 January 1950

South Africa

	First innings		Second innings	
E.A.B. Rowan	c Johnston b Miller	143	c Saggers b Lindwall	4
O.E. Wynne	b Johnston	18	b Johnson	29
J.D. Nel	c and b Johnson	14	lbw Johnston	20
A.D. Nourse	c Saggers b Johnston	66	c McCool b Johnson	27
W.W. Wade	b Lindwall	24	b Johnston	0
N.B.F. Mann	b Johnston	9	(9) lbw b Johnson	0
J.E. Cheetham	c Hassett b Johnston	4	(6) c Hassett b Johnson	1
J.C. Watkins	b Lindwall	5	(7) st Saggers b Johnson	2
H.J. Tayfield	run out	15	(8) b Johnston	3
V.I. Smith	b Lindwall	1	b Johnston	4
C.N. McCarthy	not out	0	not out	2
Sundries		12		7
		311		99

	O	M	R	W	O	M	R	W
Lindwall	19	3	47	3	4	1	7	1
Miller	24	5	73	1	7	0	12	0
McCool	13	3	35	0				
Johnston	31.2	5	75	4	18.2	6	39	4
Loxton	6	1	31	0				
Johnson	16	5	38	1	17	2	34	5

Fall of wickets
First innings: 32, 75, 242, 264, 283, 289, 293, 304, 308, 311
Second innings: 9, 51, 85, 88, 90, 93, 93, 93, 99

Australia

	First innings		Second innings	
A.R. Morris	c Smith b Tayfield	25	hit wkt b Tayfield	44
J. Moroney	b Tayfield	10	lbw b Tayfield	10
I.W. Johnson	lbw b Tayfield	2		
K.R. Miller	b Tayfield	2	(3) lbw b Mann	10
A.L. Hassett	lbw b Tayfield	2	(4) lbw b Mann	11
R.A. Saggers	c Cheetham b Mann	2		
C.L. McCool	lbw b Mann	1	not out	39
R.R. Lindwall	b Mann	7		
R.N. Harvey	c and b Tayfield	2	(5) not out	151
S.J.E. Loxton	c Cheetham b Tayfield	16	(6) b Mann	54
W.A. Johnston	not out	2		
Sundries		4		17
		75		5 for 336

	O	M	R	W	0	M	R	W
McCarthy	6	2	8	0	12	3	32	0
Watkins	4	1	9	0	6	2	10	0
Mann	10	1	31	3	51.6	13	101	3
Tayfield	8.4	1	23	.7	49	5	144	2
Smith					5	0	32	0

Fall of wickets
First innings: 31, 35, 37, 39, 42, 46, 53, 63, 75
Second innings: 14, 33, 59, 95, 230

Australia won by five wickets

BILL LAWRY

Bill Lawry goes down on one knee to whip the ball away to the boundary.

BILL LAWRY

'Yon Cassius has a lean and hungry look. He thinks too much. Such men are dangerous.' William Shakespeare, *Julius Caesar*

Tall, lean, gum-chewing and with the long nose of an echidna, Bill Lawry showed grit and guts as he steered, nudged and carved 13 Test centuries for Australia in the 1960s.

Scoring 5234 runs in his 67 Tests at a healthy average of 47.15, the left-handed Victorian was once described as the rock-solid trellis around which the public's fancy dans entwined their colourful summer blooms. Only Allan Border, Greg Chappell, Ian Chappell, Sir Donald Bradman, Doug Walters and Neil Harvey have scored more runs for Australia.

Lawry was invariably at the other end of the pitch, grim and determined as he conscientiously swept the stage for the entrance of the Harveys and O'Neills and Walters. They would not have done nearly as well without him.

With seven of his Test 100s coming against England and four against the West Indies, Lawry dug in and battled it out against the blazing fires of West Indians Charlie Griffith and Wes Hall, England's Freddie Trueman, Brian Statham and John Snow, and South Africa's Mike Proctor and Peter Pollock.

When he first came on to the Australian side in 1961, Lawry could play drives and hooks with the best of them, once carving 101 between lunch and tea on the way to 165 against Surrey at The Oval. Twice he hit three sixes on the first day of a Test match: once against the West Indies in Bridgetown, Barbados, and on another occasion against England at Old Trafford.

But once he became captain of Victoria and Australia, Lawry's outlook and batting closed up like an oyster to be much more hard-line and defensive because of his determination to avoid defeat at all costs. He was Captain Snooze, who once set the West Indies 734 to win after labouring to 151 in the first innings of a Sydney Test; a man dubbed by Ian Wooldridge as a corpse with pads on.

Lawry admits:

> Yes, I did play some shockers. I was a victim of my own attitude. Looking back, I would like to have played more attacking innings, but everything I did was what I thought was best for the team at the time. It will never be on my

conscience that I played for myself because I was very much a team player. I probably played as many attacking innings as defensive ones, but at times I got myself into too defensive a mould because I was uncertain what role to play. You can't put an old head on young shoulders.

Peter Roebuck, captain of the Somerset county team and a pithy writer on the game, sums up:

Bill was the man all England loved to hate. He was the bloke who didn't reckon he was out when his stumps were sprawled across the ground. Trouble was, this didn't happen very often and with his pinched visage and productive batting, he drove us towards dementia . . . In the end he won our hearts with his cussedness, and later he turned out to be a companionable bloke with a sound, analytical mind.

When his playing days were over, Lawry emerged from behind the pickets of the Melbourne Cricket Ground with one of the most cheerful natures that could be imagined. Of course, his team-mates had long feared the practical jokes of a man who once nailed skipper Richie Benaud's shoes to the dressing room floor. 'The best after dinner sports speaker in Australia,' says comedian Brian Doyle, who should know.

Straight man: 'If Geoff Boycott and Bill Lawry opened the innings, they could make one-day cricket last a fortnight.' To which Lawry responds: 'If Boycott and I had played together, we would have run each other out.'

As the plane carrying his 1968 Australian team circled before landing, Lawry pointed to the Tower of London, saying: 'That's where they'll want to put me — on bread and water.' After his seven-and-a-half hour 135 as Australia battled for a draw in the final Test at The Oval, he was probably right.

Lawry was once sensitive to jokes about the size of his long nose, which seems to end at his chin and could enable him to double as a sniffer dog. Now he chuckles, 'When I got the sack as Australian captain, I'll bet it was the cartoonists who cried. They draped more cobwebs and spiders between my nose and the non-striker's end than they could have with Bob Simpson and Ian Chappell.'

Born 11 September 1937 in the Melbourne suburb of Thornbury, William Morris Lawry was the second son of a tobacco stripper in a cigarette factory, but grew up not to smoke (or drink liquor). Tending the family pigeon lofts gave him a lifelong passion for the racing birds, an interest he shares with heavyweight boxer Mike Tyson and tough guy actor Clint Eastwood. During the 1961 English tour, on which he scored a stunning 2117 runs with nine centuries, Lawry was invited to the Royal pigeon loft at Windsor.

Playing in the Victorian Second XI when a gawky 17-year-old, apprentice plumber Lawry won a nickname which has stuck for life. On the train trip to Adelaide, he tucked himself into a corner with a fistful of Phantom comics. From that day on he was known as the Phantom.

Lawry joined forces with Bob Simpson to form the most productive of all Australian opening pairs. Their record 382 partnership against the devilish pace of Charlie Griffith and Wes Hall in the Bridgetown, Barbados Test against the West Indies in 1965 was the cherry on top of the cake.

Hall thundered to the wicket in great bouncing strides, a gold chain swinging across his bared chest, and the red ball in his great fist carrying the menace of a grenade. The threat of Griffith came more subtly. His run was shorter, but in the final explosion of effort he seemed to catch fire. General opinion among the Australians was that big Charlie threw the ball.

The scent of blood was in the air when a Griffith bumper gashed Lawry's cheekbone, but he and Simpson proved their courage with a stand of 382 — almost unbelievable scoring against Griffith, Hall, Gary Sobers and Lance Gibbs. Lawry's 210 lasted nine hours and included 24 fours and three sixes, still the top score by an Australian in the West Indies.

Lawry says:

> I got 13 Test 100s and enjoyed every one of them. Some were very good, some average. But unless it was a winning 100, I didn't get as much satisfaction out of it. That game at Kensington Oval finished up a draw, with both teams scoring over 600. Simmo and I were the first Test openers to score a double century in the same innings, and the partnership did a lot to boost our confidence for the future. Although it was a very good batting wicket, Hall and Griffith still were difficult, but once they were off you were down to Gary Sobers' medium-pacers and Lance Gibbs bowling off-spin.
>
> It's much tougher now playing the West Indies than in our day. They've got an armoury of four quick bowlers that has made them the best team in the world for the last 15 years. Regardless of what anybody says, fast bowlers win Test matches.
>
> We copped plenty of bouncers like the guys do now, but it's no good bitching about it. If we had the fast bowlers, we'd do it, too. Griffith's action was certainly suspect, but I don't think anyone throws the ball deliberately.

Guys like Charlie simply use the natural action they learn to bowl with and that's very unfortunate.

Of course, not every chucker is a danger man. One year Sir Donald Bradman's batting partner walked up the pitch and said, 'Hey, Don. This guy is a chucker.' Bradman replied, 'Don't say anything. They might take him off.'

I thought my best innings against the West Indies was when I got 205 in Melbourne in 1968. We'd lost the first Test in Brisbane, and I sent them in in the next Test in Melbourne. They made 200, and I replied with 205, probably the only time a captain has put the other side in and then topped their score on his own. I was 117 not out overnight and in Sobers' first over I hit a full toss straight back at him. I've never seen him spill a catch before or since, but he dropped it. That was the turning point because when something like that happens you think, well, I'm going to get a big one today. We won the Test and took the series 3–1.

When I was battling with Ian Craig and Brian Booth for the last two batting spots in the 1961 Australian team to England, Victoria played NSW in Sydney while the Test team was playing the West Indies in Melbourne. I was dropped by Ray Flockton at 12 and went on to get 266. I got a century against Queensland in the next game, but it was that big innings in Sydney that got me on the boat to England. Still, Ian Craig made his name with a double century for NSW against South Africa when he was 17 after being caught behind first ball and given not out.

However, when it came to nominating the innings that gave him the biggest buzz, Lawry bypasses the Test arena and plumps for the 1965–66 Victorian Cricket Association's district final between his beloved Northcote club and Essendon at the Albert ground. The rules called for the game to be played until a first innings result was achieved. Essendon batted first and declared at tea on the second day at nine for 514. The Essendon attack included former State bowlers John Grant and Keith Kirby.

Lawry recalls:

I'd been with Northcote since I was 11,and the club hadn't won the flag since 1912. I'd made 979 runs in seven games against Mike Smith's touring England team, and now I was back at the grass roots of the game. I was a Test player in form, the best batsman in the game, and I was expected to get the runs. But that isn't always on. I was very excited at the prospect of the long haul. In the semi-finals, Richmond bowled us out for 81, but we struck back to knock them over for 61, with Ken Walker taking 9 for 29.

Beginning the run chase against Essendon, I took a single off the first ball and my opening partner Wayne Robinson was dropped off the first delivery he faced. We finished the day 0 for 98 and went on and on and on for the next two days. At the start of the fourth day, we were 4 for 404, but passed their total for the loss of five wickets and I finished 282 not out, a record for a final.

It reminded me of a story of a district final in Adelaide in which Clarrie Grimmett's team was playing Sir Donald Bradman's in blazing century heat. Old fox Grimmett told his captain, 'If you win the toss, put them in. Don will get 180 and then get out.' Bradman got 180, threw his wicket away and they made 355. After Clarrie's team won the game, he said, 'If we'd batted first and made 450, he'd have got 400 of them himself.'

Lawry's choice of that innings will come as a surprise to aficionados because his 130 against England in 1961, in which balls kicked from a wicked ridge on the pitch at Lord's, remains one of the game's classics. Although Freddie Trueman and Brian Statham kept rattling his fingers and ribs with deliveries rearing off a length, Lawry played for six hours with dry, undemonstrative aplomb, finding unerringly the ball he could tuck away on the leg side or drive through the arc between cover-point and mid-wicket. If the ball beat his bat, he refused to become unsettled.

Seventh out at 238, Lawry had seen his side to 32 ahead. It was the Test innings of his life. Of his 130, he made 101 off the dangermen Trueman and Statham, and hit 15 of his 18 fours off them. Yet in the dressing room Lawry groaned to skipper Neil Harvey, 'We are not enough, are we?' In the end Australia won by five wickets and within an hour of the finish surveyors were at the pitch charting the ridge with their instruments.

John Arlott predicted, 'There seems little doubt that Lawry is destined to take his place among the major batsmen of Test history. Phlegmatic, shrewd, courageous, with hands sensitive to the bat, he showed a degree of maturity quite amazing in one who was playing in only his second Test. Certainly he is no mere good wicket player, for he faced freak pace superbly.'

With becoming modesty, Lawry says:

I've played on wickets that have done a lot more and I've certainly made centuries that were much better. I played and missed a lot and luck was with me. Other times you can nick the first ball and you're gone. Still, I suppose it was a courageous knock for a guy in only his second Test. It established me in the Australian side rather than being a guy just trying to stay in the team, much as Mark Taylor was before he got a century in the first English Test in 1989.

At one end the bounce wasn't even and the ball took off occasionally off the ridge. This upset the real stroke-players rather than a defensive guy like me. Personally, I don't think the bowlers got enough credit. Alan Davidson and Graham McKenzie bowled superbly for us and Freddie Trueman and Brian Statham bowled well for England.

We won that Test and as I said before, you tend to remember the winning 100s. The fourth Test of that 1961 series at Manchester was the first time Bobby Simpson and I batted together. Trailing by 177 after the first innings, Simmo and I put on 113 to put us back into the game. I was dropped at 32 by Subba Row at slip off Trueman and that was a turning point because I finished with 102 and we won the most exciting Test match I ever played in by 54 runs. There were some sensational individual performances on the last day. Davo and McKenzie's last wicket partnership of 98, Ted Dexter on fire and Richie Benaud spinning them out. We really shouldn't have won it, but Richie bluffed them by going round the wicket to bowl into the footmarks. He took six wickets and there were a couple of magnificent slips catches by Simmo.

With Simpson's premature retirement in 1967, the selectors made Lawry Australian skipper. He held the job for 25 Tests until the axe fell before the final Test of the 1970–71 series against the touring Englishmen. With his nerves stretched taut, his last nine Tests as captain had produced five losses and four draws, but Bill deserved much better than first hearing he had been dumped over the radio.

Lawry's tight-fisted intensity as skipper led him to argue with umpires, sharply rebuke his bowlers if they gave up runs and slap his pad in frustration at the sight of a batting partner's dangerous shot. In other words, the poor fellow just couldn't relax.

His single-mindedness as Australian captain is best emphasised by his reactions during the riot in the 1969 Bombay Test, when crazed spectators set fire to the stand and hurled hundreds of bottles onto the field in protest against an Indian batsman being given out near the end of the day. With riot squad police attempting to suppress the rioters, the game eventually continued. 'Kill Lawry, kill Lawry,' chanted the crowd.

Between overs, vice-captain Ian Chappell told Lawry, 'At stumps, I think we should gather in the middle of the ground and leave as a team. That'll be a lot safer than walking off individually.'

When there was no reply, Chappell looked across to see if Lawry had heard. 'What do you think, Phant?'

'Christ, we need a wicket bad,' was Lawry's grunted reply.

Bill Lawry was an unyielding sheet anchor of Australia's innings for a decade, with innings of 210 and 205 against the West Indies among the 13 centuries and 27 half-centuries in his portfolio of 5234 Test runs.

Apart from his 382 record opening stand with Bob Simpson against the Windies, he joined forces with Simpson in a 244 first wicket partnership against England in Adelaide in 1965–66.

How the West Indian bowlers must have hated his broad blade, as Lawry figured in record partnerships against them of 298 with Ian Chappell in Melbourne for the second wicket, then 336 with Doug Walters in Sydney for the fourth wicket in the 1968–69 series.

When the going got tough, Lawry dropped anchor and clung to the crease like a limpet. His unbeaten 60 out of Australia's 116 against England in Sydney in 1970 was the second time he had batted through a Test innings.

Lawry comments:

> I was an opener from the time I started going in first with the Sunday School team. I never wanted to play anywhere else. You might have to go in after spending a lot of time in the field, but if you're an opener you get the chance to bat through the innings and really do something for the team. It's better than going in at 2 for 2 or 1 for 190 when you're expected to carve the attack up.
>
> Bobby Simpson and I respected each other's ability and, I can say this, we were very good runners between wickets. You get established as a pair and the press begins to play on it. The opposition sits down and says, 'How do you get these guys out?' With a partner like Simmo, it's a lot easier than if you've got a nervous starter at the other end who you've got to protect.
>
> I loved to take the first ball of an innings, but we shared it. It's an advantage to take strike because the bowler hasn't bowled a ball and is just as keyed up as you are. You're likely to get an ordinary ball in the first two or three. It's a bit like the footballer who wants to get a touch of the ball as quickly as possible. Besides, the bowler always looks faster from the non-striker's end. It's better to go in at 0 for 0 than 1 for 10 when the bowler has got his tail up.
>
> Don't believe the talk that Simmo played more shots than I did because he didn't. Okay, I played a few shockers, but if you look at the stats you'll see that he hit many more singles than I did. The press forms an opinion of a guy and I was the one with cobwebs draped all over him.
>
> An opener can play a sensational innings if he sticks in there for 35 in the first session when the ball is seaming around. The guy then gets out after lunch after doing the hard slog. In comes Charlie Charisma who scores 150 and at the end of the day everyone says how brilliant he was. Still, that's what a team sport is all about.

Since putting away his bat and cricketing creams, Lawry has become a super-enthusiastic TV cricket commentator with a knack of livening up proceedings with a waspish comment to Tony Greig, or by delivering such gems as: 'He wants to middle one or two balls in the centre of his bat.' When not doing cricket commentary or racing his pigeons, Bill can be found carrying out his duties as the Victorian Cricket Association's cricket manager.

ESSENDON v NORTHCOTE
Albert Ground, April 1966

Essendon

I. Monks c Lawry b Ryan	136
R. Howe c Walker b Mitton	0
D. Foster b Shanahan	31
J. Swanson c Morrison b Shanahan	23
G. Brown run out	36
J. Grant c Morrison b Shanahan	39
J. Peters c Morrison b Shanahan	54
B. Davies c Gosstray b Walker	61
T. O'Neill b Mitton	67
K. Kirby not out	50
K. Adams not out	3
Sundries	14
	9 (dec) for 514

	0	M	R	W
Walker	29	0	95	1
Mitton	21	2	105	2
Brew	25	1	113	0
Shanahan	34	1	143	4
Ryan	12	2	37	1
Lawry	1	0	7	0

Fall of wickets: 2, 124, 165, 205, 253, 283, 363, 430, 491

Northcote

W. Lawry not out	282
W. Robinson lbw b Kirby	41
R. Gosstray lbw b Grant	23
L. Cowley c Davis b Adams	5
T. Ryan c Monks b Adams	82
F. Brew c Adams b Grant	47
P. Burn not out	0
Sundries	36
	5 for 516

	O	M	R	W
Grant	31	3	134	2
Adams	25	3	105	2
Kirby	35.1	4	135	1
Swanson	20	4	49	0
Peters	2	0	14	0
Davis	4	0	22	0
Howe	5	0	21	0

Fall of wickets: 130, 206, 219, 411, 505

Northcote won on first innings

NORMAN O'NEILL

Norm O'Neill, who struck the ball gloriously to hit six Test centuries, strides out to bat.

NORMAN O'NEILL

I get the feeling Norman O'Neill would like to strangle the idiot who first pinned the tag of the new Don Bradman to his reluctant chest.

'Was I an enigma?' asks O'Neill, the NSW player who struck the ball gloriously in scoring six picket-peppering centuries in his 42 Tests, which produced 2779 runs at the highly respectable average of 45.56. 'I take it as it comes. People can make up their own minds.

'I had this stigma of being called another Bradman. People expected me to get centuries. When I failed or got a duck, it was headlines. I was supposed to finish with a Test batting average of 99.94 like Don did, and that's just not on. I wasn't a good starter, but once I settled down I just played my shots.'

The 'new Bradman' tag proved deadlier than a gypsy's curse, and at times distorted O'Neill's status and achievements. Still, he has no regrets about a career in which his powerful stroke-play linked him with the West Indies' Gary Sobers, England's Ted Dexter, and South Africa's Graeme Pollock, as the world's most exciting batsmen of the era.

At the start of an innings O'Neill could be as nervous as a swarm of bees, but when he controlled his emotions and curbed the early jittery shots that often led to his downfall, he could be unstoppable. He hit a wide range of shots tremendously hard, particularly off the back foot.

O'Neill was top-scorer with 181 in the fabulous 1960 tied Test against the West Indies in Brisbane. During his 117 against England at The Oval in 1961 he carved 45 runs in half an hour while Peter Burge, himself a powerful hitter of the ball, was scoring three.

Left elbow studiously high, O'Neill attacked the bowling with a lovely exuberance and gave the impression of having so much strength to spare that batting was hardly enough for him. In the field, particularly in the covers, his telescopic arm flicked out like a lizard's tongue to pluck the ball from the air; his bazooka-like throwing was sharpened by baseball. No wonder the New York Yankees tried to steal him away.

O'Neill was one of those charismatic people who couldn't keep out of the headlines. It didn't matter whether he was making a duck or a century or marrying Gwen Wallace, the stunning Australian athlete who won a gold medal at the 1954 Empire Games. They called her the Pocket Venus.

If ever anyone looked a cricketer, it was Norm O'Neill. He was a handsome, dark-haired, blue-eyed fellow, etched bronze by the Australian sun and with a powerful shoulder and arm.

He was the sort of player people loved to watch and argue about. His decision to retire in April 1967 due to crippling bone growths in his knees was a blow to Australian cricket.

Born 19 February 1937 in the Sydney suburb of Carlton, where his father was a master builder, young Norm used to enthusiastically practise his shots in the garden by continually hitting at a ball enclosed in a stocking hung from a clothes line.

As a youngster, he joined the local St George club, whose previous champions included Don Bradman, Bill O'Reilly, Ray Lindwall and Arthur Morris. After being bowled for a duck in his first game for NSW at the age of 18, O'Neill won a place in an Australian team for a tour of New Zealand in 1957 on the strength of a single season of first class cricket. In the unofficial Test, he upstaged Neil Harvey, Bobby Simpson and Richie Benaud by scoring 102 not out. In those days, New Zealand wasn't considered worthy of official Test status.

O'Neill seemed a certainty for the Australian trip to South Africa in 1957–58 and there was an outcry when the selectors left him out. They could only sit with red faces as he carved up the other States in a manner which overshadowed the Test team battling it out with the Springboks.

The pinnacle of that devastating season came at the Sydney Cricket Ground when O'Neill struck 38 fours in an innings of 233 in 244 minutes against Victoria. The fans had seen nothing like it since the heyday of the Don, and overnight he was labelled an embryonic Bradman.

By the end of the summer O'Neill had piled up 1005 runs for the season, the first time a NSW player had passed the 1000 mark, at an average of 83.75. In those days there were only eight Sheffield Shield matches a season. Just for good measure, Norm took 26 wickets with his spinners to head the Shield bowling averages, too.

Thus the stage was set for the 100 which O'Neill cherishes more than any of the 46 centuries he made with such panache in the first class arena. He recalls:

> There was a lot of interest in how I'd shape against a top world-class attack, and the publicity was unbelievable when I was invited to play in a Combined XI against Peter May's touring English team in Perth in 1958. Colin McDonald and Slasher Mackay were in the Combined team, too. They'd both been to South Africa, with Slasher coming home with the batting average. I was just 21 years old.
>
> At first it's nice to open up the papers to find the journos wrapping you, but after a while this really put the pressure on. Freddie Trueman, Brian Statham, Jim Laker and Peter Loader threw the lot at me. I got word the Poms had been

saying on the ship coming over that they'd fix me up in a matter of five minutes.

I was down to bat at four when our skipper John Rutherford and Colin McDonald opened the batting after MCC made 349 and I had the pads on just in case as they put on 40-odd. I used to bowl a lot of wrong 'uns, so when Rutherford dropped his bat, did the wrong 'un bit and pointed at the dressing room, it was a signal that when the first wicket fell, I was in.

I opened with a couple of fours off Laker and played quite well that day to finish with 80 not out. When I came in, Slasher and Col McDonald came over without any fuss and said, 'Now we've seen it for ourselves. You can bat, son.' That gave me a really big kick.

Freddie Trueman was a wild man in those days. The Perth wicket was very quick and he hurled a barrage of bumpers at me. I was a non-hooker in those days, and I ended up on my backside trying to avoid a few of them. Once Freddie came charging down. 'I thought thee bloody well hooked,' he snorted, adding a few other words for good measure.

That night I got a phone call from Sir Donald Bradman, who asked if he could see me the next morning. He came and very generously said, 'Well played.' Don then said he considered off spinner Laker the danger man in the coming series, particularly when they got to the turning wickets in the eastern States.

'When you've got your 100,' he said, 'I want you to go after Laker. Go with the turn and punch him through the mid-wicket and mid-on areas.' Although I needed another 20 for my century, Don took it as a matter of course that I'd get them. It was quite a compliment.

I got to 104 and was promptly caught by Colin Cowdrey at slip off Laker, so I never got after him. It had been a bit of a struggle, but that innings meant a lot to me. It was the one that really got me started in Test cricket.

As a follow-up to that baptism of fire, O'Neill played a most significant innings in Brisbane to tip the first Test Australia's way. Chasing 146 to win amid rumours of an impending storm on the last day of the match, O'Neill, cutting and driving off the back foot with majesty, hit 71 not out from 89 for the third wicket, enabling Australia to win by eight wickets.

O'Neill says, 'You forget about some of the innings if you didn't get the three figures, but after that one I knew I was going to play in five Tests. It confirmed my place in the Australian side.'

In the Test series, he averaged 56.40 and played a major role in the recapture of the Ashes. It was not merely the runs; it was the way he scored them. Commented Wisden: 'In O'Neill, Australia found a new star with old-fashioned ideas of using the bat for the main purpose of hitting the ball.'

Then it was off to India and Pakistan for a triumphant tour. On that tour he ripped off 163 and 113 against India at Bombay and Calcutta respectively, 134 against Pakistan at Lahore and a career best 284 against a President's XI in India.

O'Neill recalls:

> It was a pretty hard tour because the living conditions weren't what they are today. At times it was a drag for guys like Ray Lindwall, who'd been around for a long time.
>
> Apart from New Zealand, it was my first trip overseas and I loved it. Every day was a new challenge.
>
> It was bloody hot in India and Pakistan, so any local thinking of becoming a fast bowler in those days had to be some sort of nut. It's different now because they play so much more cricket away from home. There is more incentive for guys to take the long run-up.
>
> In those days it was basically tight, accurate bowling by medium pacers and spinners to good field placements. Spin played a big part in the game, and at times it was difficult.
>
> I couldn't stick around and wait and wait and wait because I wasn't that sort of player. I had to go after the bowling, otherwise it would have been boring for myself and the crowd. Neil Harvey liked to play exactly the same way, and I couldn't get enough chances to bat with him. I loved it, although I found it difficult at first when the crowd began to chant as the bowler ran up to the wicket.
>
> The game with the President's XI on the mat at Ahmedabed gave us a chance for revenge against off spinner Jasu Patel, who only a week earlier had cleaned us out by taking 14 wickets on a turning turf wicket at Kanpur to give India its first ever victory over Australia. He ended up with the equivalent of a knighthood.
>
> When we went after him in the President's XI game, Patel tried to push the ball through and dig it in, but he was gone. After 20 overs or so, he left the field injured and didn't come back.

O'Neill began the 1960 Test series against the West Indies with his highest-ever Test score of 181 with 22 fours in Brisbane, during which he was struck many times by Wes Hall's thunderbolts. Jack Fingleton commented: 'His first 50 had the taste of corked wine; the second bubbled like champagne, if one overlooks his extreme good fortune in the fifties. His last 100 runs were replete with red meat.'

O'Neill recalls:

> It was a pretty hard grind. The longest innings I ever played, lasting exactly 400 minutes. Still, you didn't really have time to try to tear them apart. Wes Hall was taking up to ten minutes to bowl an eight-ball over and three or four of them could be bouncers. There was no restriction on the number of bouncers you could bowl in an over, and Wes just loved bowling them. He was the quickest bowler I've ever seen.
>
> Wes would be on your chest all day, with no restriction of fieldsmen on the leg side. You had to be careful with the hook shot or turning the ball off your hip.
>
> Look at a guy like Neil Harvey, one of the greatest players of all time. He didn't average in the 60s like they're doing now. The changes of rules have been all in favour of the batsman. Helmets, a restriction of bouncers and the number of fieldsmen on the leg side. Myself, I'm not too sure about the helmets. They seem to be cumbersome and restrict movement.
>
> In the old days, 350 or 400 was a good first innings total and it gave you a good chance to win the match. Not now, though. I'm not saying they don't bowl as well these days or that the guys can't bat. Even Bradman has said he would find it a lot more difficult to score as quickly these days than he did when he was breaking all the batting records.

O'Neill's Test career came to a close when he branded Charlie Griffith a chucker after Australia's 1965 tour of the West Indies. Nari Contractor, the Indian batsman, had to undergo a six-hour brain operation after being struck by a ball from Griffith, who bore a striking resemblance to the late Sonny Liston, the world heavyweight boxing champion. At times Griffith could hurl thunderbolts of almost unbelievable pace.

O'Neill's final Test innings at Bridgetown, Barbados, brought him 74 not out in a run chase which included two huge sixes over the grandstand off Lance Gibbs and a broken finger courtesy of old rival Wes Hall. On that trip, Norm topped the first class averages with 68.55 and four centuries, but vowed he would never again play against the West Indies. Noting this outburst, the selectors left him out of the Australian team to play in South Africa in 1966.

O'Neill has no regrets over labelling Griffith as a cheat who wilfully threw a cricket ball instead of bowling it. He says:

> Charlie threw. Everyone knew he did. Richie Benaud came up with some photos that proved he was one of the worst chuckers of all time. The big thing about Griffith was that the pace of his bowling could change so rapidly. He

> wasn't quick all the time. In a six-ball over, you might get three that weren't too much over medium pace. Because of the low trajectory at which he bowled, any bounced ball skidded off the wicket and was on you before you realised what was happening. If he didn't chuck a bouncer, he'd hurl one right at the blockhole.

What isn't generally known is that O'Neill once had a plane ticket in his hand to fly to America for a tryout with the New York Yankees, the most famous baseball club of them all. He reveals:

> It was just after I turned down a job offer from Adelaide, and I was very happy because you like to stick with your home State. During the 1958–59 Test against England in Melbourne, I was approached by Billy Talbert, the American Davis Cup tennis captain, on behalf of the New York Yankees. We met again in Sydney and I was offered very good money to try out with the Yankees and then be placed. Of course, I'm not suggesting I would have gone straight into the top team, but the chance was there. Talbert even gave me a plane ticket.
>
> Rothmans were very good. I'd just signed a 10-year contract, but they left it up to me. Sir Ronald Irish, the head man at Rothmans in those days, loved his cricket and I think he wanted to keep me in the game. He told me to be careful, and after talking with Talbert he said bluntly, 'The young fellow's not coming.' Two hours later my flight to New York was cancelled.

After he quit big cricket, Norm O'Neill spent 12 years in Perth where he ran a successful cricket coaching school. Returning to Sydney, he moved into an idyllic spot at Phegans Bay near Gosford, where it takes him just an hour to get to Rothmans, where he is Community Services Executive. O'Neill stayed in the game doing radio commentary with the ABC, and has several times been in the box when son Mark has scored centuries for Western Australia and NSW.

O'Neill is the most modest of champions, and son Mark says, 'Dad hasn't got any cricket memorabilia around the house. It's all locked away in his memory.' When the old family dog was feeling cold one freezing night, Norm simply went to an old trunk and took a few jumpers for the dog to sleep on. Australian cricket jumpers.

O'Neill may have been nervy at the start of an innings, but what the hell. The man was entertainment plus and the crowds adored him. Give me half an hour watching O'Neill playing his handsome strokes or fielding in the covers and you can have all the run-hungry players who treat every ball as it if was a bomb likely to explode at the slightest hint of violence.

Norm O'Neill's only regret is that he couldn't have squeezed another three or four years out of his cricket career. 'There is just one thing that would make me completely happy,' he says. 'One day I would like to be remembered as Mark O'Neill's dad.'

MCC v COMBINED XI
Perth, 24–28 October 1958

MCC

P.E. Richardson c Rutherford b Slater........4	c sub b Strauss 5
C.A. Milton c Rutherford b Slater 15	c Watson b O'Neill........8
R. Subba Row c Watson b Strauss............14	b Simpson........15
P.B.H. May c McDonald b Strauss..........113	
M.C. Cowdrey c Simpson b Rutherford ..78	not out........100
T.E. Bailey b Strauss.........17	not out........71
T.G. Evans c Watson b Strauss.........55	
J.C. Laker b Strauss 2	
F.S. Trueman c Simpson b O'Neill..........13	c Simpson b Rutherford........53
J.B. Statham c sub b Rutherford 16	
P.J. Loader not out........11	
349	4 for 257

	O	M	R	W	O	M	R	W
Slater	23	7	81	2	18	5	52	0
Hoare	9	2	33	0				
O'Neill	11	1	47	1	3	0	20	1
Strauss	22	1	99	5	12	6	24	1
Germaine	6	0	38	0	20	2	65	0
Rutherford	11.2	5	17	2	10	2	39	1
Mackay	9	2	23	0				
Simpson					11	4	36	1
Shepherd					2	0	5	0
McDonald					2	0	11	0

Fall of wickets
First innings: 6, 33, 33, 201, 211, 303, 307, 308, 336, 349
Second innings: 9, 37, 78, 91

Combined XI

C.C. McDonald c Cowdrey b Laker.........27
J. Rutherford c Evans b Statham 34
N. O'Neill c Cowdrey b Laker 104
R. Simpson b Statham..........17
K. Mackay run out..........10
B. Shepherd b Loader..........24
K. Slater lbw Loader 2
R. Watson not out..........24
D. Hoare b Loader 0
R. Strauss b Loader..........14
L. Germaine run out 2
Sundries 2
260

	O	M	R	W
Trueman	20	2	63	0
Statham	19	6	35	2
Loader	21.3	4	56	4
Laker	26	7	55	2
Bailey	9	2	26	0
Milton	1	0	23	0

Fall of wickets: 39, 92, 168, 197, 199, 202, 225, 227, 251, 260

Match drawn

ALAN DAVIDSON

Alan Davidson smashes a soaring six during his epic innings against England at Old Trafford.

ALAN DAVIDSON

'If I had one ball hanging between me and death, I'd give it to Alan Davidson.' Bob Simpson

As a left-handed opening bowler for Australia, Alan Davidson was a dangerous, cunning fellow who cut and swung the ball late in either direction with glorious rhythm to capture 186 wickets in his 44 Tests before retiring while still at the peak of his powers.

Broad-shouldered and beetle-browed, he doubled as a phenomenal fieldsman, nicknamed The Claw by his peers, and a middle-order batsman who could hit soaring, steepling sixes in a manner of which small boys dream. Davo was simply one of the finest all-round cricketers the world has seen, as evidenced by his 11 wickets and 124 runs in the fantastic tied Test against the West Indies in Brisbane in 1960. In fact, if he had not concentrated on bowling to such an extent, he could well have become a specialist Test batsman in his own right.

'How great a batsman Alan might have been had not bowling taken up so much of his energy,' Sir Donald Bradman observed when Davidson quit Test cricket in 1963 after snaring five English wickets for 25 at the Sydney Cricket Ground. 'I can't think of any all-round cricketer whose absence from the Australian XI was of more importance.'

Davidson himself has no doubts he could have made it to the top purely as a batsman. As a young man, he claims his eyesight was so sharp that when the ball was coming through the air, he could pick which side the kookaburra logo was on.

Although often batting as low as number nine, Davidson scored ten centuries for Australia and NSW, with the cherry on top of the cake being his 157 not out for the Australian Second XI against Wairarapa in Masterton, New Zealand, as a follow-up to a first day haul of 10 wickets for 29.

A search through ancient and dusty records found Wisden's only other instances of such a feat occurred way back in 1859, when V.E. Walker took 10 for 74 and scored 108 runs; in 1862 when E.M. Grace batted through the innings for 192 and then took ten wickets in the second innings of a 12-a-side match; and in 1886 when W.G. Grace made 104 runs and took 10 for 49.

Davo's powers of recall are legendary, and he describes the two days which stunned the cricketing world:

It was a greenish wicket, and at one stage I had 8 for 11. Our captain Billy Brown walked across and asked: 'Have you ever taken ten wickets in an innings before?' When I shook my head, he said, 'Well, you've got another two overs. Give it a go.'

The harder I tried, the worse I bowled. At the other end the batsman swung at our other opening bowler, Len Johnson, who'd held the ball back, and the catch went straight up in the air. Lennie got underneath for the caught and bowled, but he spilled it. They told me later he'd dropped the catch on purpose so I could take all ten wickets, but I'm not so sure. The ball split the webbing of Lennie's hand and stitches were needed.

I picked up the ninth guy and with one ball left of my final over, I tried to bowl a really fast yorker. It turned out to be the fastest bouncer I could have bowled and it damn near cleaned the fellow up. Frantically trying to get out of the way, he trod on his wicket and that's how I got my 10 for 29.

We lost a few wickets and at the end of the day I was 70 not out batting in company with Bill Brown, who'd dropped himself down the order. When told no trace could be found in the record books of a player taking ten wickets and then scoring a century, I never slept a wink.

Batting with Bill the next morning, we kept playing shots and I raced along to 99. There was a bloke at deep mid-off to this medium pacer, so I hit the ball in his direction and took off for the single. When I got to the bowler's end, there was the captain leaning on his bat. 'Get back there,' he ordered. 'Hit a four and do it in style.' I scrambled back to beat the return to the keeper, and two balls later the bowler dropped one a bit short and I pulled it in front of square leg for a four.

When Bill Brown got out, Len Johnson came in and flogged the bowling to get a century in only 46 minutes, while I went on to finish with 157 not out. It wasn't until we came off that it rocketed home what I'd done. I went into a state of shock.

A country boy from Lisarow near Gosford, the man they called Al Pal toured England with Lindsay Hassett's 1953 Australian team, but it wasn't until after Ray Lindwall and Keith Miller quit the scene that he was allowed full scope with the new ball instead of being condemned to come on when the shine had all but disappeared.

Davidson became Australia's bowling spearhead in South Africa in 1957 and was Richie Benaud's trump card against Peter May's 1958–59 English tourists. Swerving, seaming, seething with vim, verve and menace, he ripped the heart out of the English batting in Melbourne by capturing the wickets of Peter Richardson, Willie Watson and Tom Graveney for none in the second over of the match.

No one loves cricket more than Davidson, who sums up his batting talents thus:

> My value to the side was taking the vital wickets. It was up to me to get a breakthrough against the openers and pick up a few more wickets when the new ball became due. My idea of a perfect Test match was to take five wickets and then whip up a quick 40 or 50.
>
> If Bill Lawry, Bobby Simpson, Neil Harvey and Norm O'Neill did their job up front, I didn't have to go out and get 100. Forty or 50 in an hour wasn't going to knock me about. If I didn't waste too much energy crashing the ball around the paddock, I'd have plenty left when the other side batted. However, if we were in strife, I could put the head down and, funnily enough, 90 per cent of the time it came off.

It is fitting that Davidson's favourite century occurred at the Sydney Cricket Ground, where he performed some of his mightiest deeds. With NSW at 9 for 325 against arch rivals Victoria in the 1961–62 season, Davo was joined by wicketkeeper Doug Ford. He recalls:

> It was one of those late season matches in which the Sheffield Shield was still very much up for grabs. Victoria had scored 321 and we desperately needed more runs. We had a great side in those days. In fact, Doug Ford was the only non-international.
>
> I was 48 when Doug came in and I loved facing up to that rescue type of situation. It was a bit of a circus as I raced to 106 in only 23 minutes. We put on 59 runs, with Doug facing only three balls and getting a leg bye off one of them. Their attack included Ian Meckiff, Ron Gaunt, Lindsay Kline and Colin Guest, all Test men, but it didn't matter who was bowling. I went after them and everything just clicked.
>
> The more they tried to stop the flow, the more holes I found. They'd put blokes back on the fence, and I'd chip the ball between them. I played lofted shots, too, and Doug ran brilliantly between the wickets to help break them up with singles. There weren't any sixes because I saved those up for the Poms. I had the ball on a string and somehow I always seemed able to work the ball for a single off the last ball of the over.
>
> Finally I holed out to extra cover off Guest when I'd got to 106. It was quite an incredible innings, and when Doug came in, he announced: 'That rotten bugger, Davo. He wouldn't give me the strike.' We won the match, too. That was the main thing.

Wisden's Cricketers Almanack described Davidson's heroics as 'an innings of massive power and shrewd judgment'.

I suggested to Davo that one-day cricket could well have been created to showcase a player of his exceptional all-round gifts. 'It would have been easy for me,' he said without an atom of boastfulness. 'I think I would have been able to control things. The thing about one-day cricket is that you don't have to slog. It's amazing how many runs you can pick up off an over just by keeping your head and playing sensible cricket. Richie Benaud and I proved that when we had our big partnership on the last day of the tied Test against the West Indies.'

Davidson carved himself a further niche in cricketing history by capturing 5 for 135 and 6 for 87, as well as hammering 44 and 80 run-out in that tied Test in Brisbane in 1960, which was beyond credibility. The nation came to a standstill, with millions glued to car radios and transistors.

Jack Fingleton, the doyen of cricket writers, was moved to write of Davo's second innings: 'It was a masterpiece. The West Indians chivalrously clapped the gallant Australian all the way back to the pavilion. Few greater Test innings, considering the accumulating tension and responsibility, have been played anywhere.' Davidson recalls:

> Chasing 232, we came together at 6 for 92, and with two eight-ball overs left, we needed nine runs to win with four wickets in hand. I said, 'Listen Rich, we don't have to do anything silly, but make sure I've got Wes Hall in the last over.' I reckoned Wes would bounce me, and at that time I wasn't afraid of any bloke bouncing. It was either a four or a six.
>
> Richie did not score off the first four balls from Gary Sobers. Then off the next ball he turned one straight to Joe Solomon wide of square leg and took off. If I had been Ben Johnson loaded with steroids, I still wouldn't have made that run and was three or four yards out when Joe hit the stumps. I was terribly disappointed when I got back to the room, even though I couldn't see any way we weren't going to win.
>
> When we lost three wickets, including two run-outs, in Hall's fantastic final over, the game ended in Test cricket's first-ever tie. Sir Donald Bradman came over and said: 'Well, Alan, don't be too disappointed because you've made history.' That gave me the lift I needed as the champagne corks popped.
>
> Still, although I'd made history by becoming the first Test cricketer to take ten wickets and score 100 runs in a match, and the following season I captured 7 for 31 and hit up 108 for NSW against Western Australia in Perth, the main objective for me was always to win the game.
>
> There are lots of fair-weather players that have played for Australia in my

> time and since. Great averages and great images, but fair dinkum, if I had to pick my side they wouldn't get a look in. If they get a real flat track, these guys will go out and score 300 against the Blind Society, but the moment the ball does something, no thanks, they don't want to be around. That's why I take my hat off to blokes like Ian Chappell and Neil Harvey. For them, it didn't matter what the wicket was like.

Like many others, Davidson discounts the fact that Betty Wilson was the first Test cricketer to take ten wickets and score 100 runs in a match.

Davidson's batting potential was in full bloom on Australia's 1957–58 tour of South Africa when he scored 100 against Transvaal, 100 not out against Rhodesia, 121 against Natal (while figuring in the sixth wicket stand of 244 with Richie Benaud), and 129 against Western Province, needing only 79 minutes to get to the century in the latter innings.

Casting his mind back to the Western Province century, Davo comments:

> Gee, I enjoyed that one. They had a bloke called Van Ryneveld, who'd played rugby for South Africa. He really fancied himself, and I thought, 'I'd love to play football against you, mate. I'd give you some hurry up.' He had big wraps on himself as a bowler, so I hit him over the car park into the rugby stand next door. They had another bloke called Stein, a left-handed Jimmy Burke type who pinged them. I hit him over point for six off a wide. I was charging him, so he lobbed the ball so wide it didn't land on the actual pitch.

Davidson's biggest hit occurred in the NSW versus England game at his beloved Sydney Cricket Ground when he howitzered a Colin Cowdrey leg spinner onto the dome on the roof of the old Brewongle Stand. When Tom Graveney, one of three fieldsmen on the leg boundary, heard Cowdrey yell 'Catch it,' he burst out laughing. The ball was a whizzing blur still climbing as it cleared the fence and would have been well and truly in the first deck of the new stand.

On another occasion Davidson hit Victorian off spinner Ian Johnson straight onto the top deck of the M.A. Noble Stand after failing to get to the pitch of the ball as he went down the wicket. 'I found myself short,' Davo said, 'so I just followed through. I've really hit it. It's gone a million miles high, and finished halfway up the first deck.'

'Did you see where his feet were?' Johnson said peevishly. Doug Ring, the leg spinner who'd bowled manfully against Arthur Morris, Sid Barnes and Keith Miller, only to be taken off when the tail-enders came in, said to his skipper with a grin: 'I don't know where his feet were, but by jeez, I know where the ball's finished.'

As Sir Donald Bradman pointed out, Davidson had made cricketing history with his deeds in the Brisbane tied Test, but the man himself claims he got a bigger buzz from the improbable victory in the fourth Test against England in Manchester in 1961.

Batting first, Australia struggled to 190 thanks to 74 from opener Bill Lawry. England replied with 367, and with Lawry producing a fighting 102 Australia began the final day at 6 for 331 and an overall lead of 154. Over to Davo:

I walked out for the start of the last day's play with my room-mate Slasher Mackay, who was munching away on his customary four packets of PK chewing gum. My back had been giving me a hell of a lot of trouble, and I spent an hour on the massage table before taking the field. David Allen, the off spinner, came on immediately to bowl around the wicket into the rough foot marks and Slasher pushed his second ball straight to slip.

Richie Benaud was next. He pushed the first couple of balls up the wicket and then went back to one that straightened and was plumb leg before. Wally Grout tried to win the match with one hit and holed out to deep mid-off. We'd lost three wickets for three runs to have a lead of just 157 with one wicket left.

Graham McKenzie walked through the gate. He had just turned 20 and was playing in only his third Test, so I walked across for a fatherly chat. I needn't have bothered. Here was Garth whistling away as if he was taking his dog for a walk on the beach at Cottesloe. The kid didn't have a worry in the world.

'Well, mate,' I said, 'It's up to us now. Just play straight.' Garth could play well, provided he played straight. To keep him away from the spin, I played six maidens in a row from Allen and left him to play straight to Ted Dexter.

Soon the adrenalin was pumping, so I decided to go after Allen, who was bowling into the rough and turned away from me. First ball I went down the track and pinged him over mid-off for six. I hit the third ball first bounce into the crowd just wide of the sight screen. Ten off three balls. Not surprisingly, Allen threw the following ball a bit wider and I tried to smash him through the covers, but a bloke dived full length and stopped it. I had them sprawling everywhere, and off the fifth ball I went bang and pierced the cover field for four.

What would Allen do now? Would he bowl one wide? No he won't, I thought. He'll bowl the straighty and bowl it in tight. I read it perfectly, danced into the ball and hoisted it over mid-off. It was a massive sixer, one of the sweetest I've hit in my life. If it hadn't hit the outer brick wall, it would have finished in the railway yards.

> Garth and I got rid of Freddie Trueman and Brian Statham with the new ball and had put on 98 when they brought back Jack Flavell, who was pedestrian compared with the other two. Up he came, and would you believe it, he ducked one in towards Garth's pads, the ball ricocheted off one pad onto the other and rolled onto the stumps. I was left with 77 not out. When we got back to the room everybody was very excited, so I said: 'Let's go out and knock the buggers over.'

Describing Davidson's 6, 4, 4, 6 off Allen, John Arlott said: 'These were not wild, slogger's strokes, but superbly made, measured strokes of immense power and perfect timing. It is hard to over-praise these two batsmen in playing Australia from rout to strength. Davidson batted with the cold precision of a master Test cricketer in what proved to be a match-winning innings.'

With England needing to score 256 at a rate of 66 an hour, Davidson shrugged off his back troubles to get rid of England opener Geoff Pullar. Ted Dexter savaged the Australian bowling for 76 before Benaud went round the wicket to bowl his leg breaks into the rough. Dexter was promptly caught at the wicket by Grout cutting and Peter May was bowled round his legs attempting to sweep his second ball. Slasher Mackay ignored a torn calf muscle to bowl Ken Barrington and Bobby Simpson grabbed a couple of amazing slip catches. Benaud had 6 for 70 when Davidson fittingly uprooted Statham's stumps to give Australia a stunning victory by 54 runs.

Many Test cricketers melt into comparative obscurity when their playing days are over, but Alan Davidson has remained firmly in the public eye. A Member of the British Empire for services to cricket and NSW Father of the Year in 1982, he seems to have been Executive Director of the Rothmans Sports Foundation almost for as long as anyone can remember. Davo was an Australian selector, and has been President of the NSW Cricket Association for more than 20 years. He is also a Member of the Order of Australia.

NSW v VICTORIA

Sydney, 12–16 January 1962

Victoria

W. Lawry c Misson b Simpson	97	b Benaud 67
D. Anderson b Davidson	0	c Craig b Davidson 0
R. Furlong c and b Martin	82	c O'Neill b Simpson 26
J. Potter c Benaud b Davidson	53	c Ford b Martin 12
R. Cowper not out	64	c O'Neill b Simpson 18
N. Crompton c Ford b Simpson	2	b Benaud 27
R. Jordon c Ford b Martin	3	b Martin 3
C. Guest st Ford b Martin	5	c O'Neill b Benaud 27
L. Kline c Davidson b Simpson	5	c Booth b Simpson 2
I. Meckiff run out	6	b Benaud 0
R. Gaunt c and b Martin	0	not out 0
Sundries	4	16
	321	198

	O	M	R	W	O	M	R	W
Davidson	16	1	63	2	3	0	8	1
Misson	23	4	72	0	3	0	9	0
Booth	4	1	10	0				
Martin	30.1	8	80	4	24	4	85	2
Benaud	9	1	24	0	19.3	5	49	4
Simpson	27	7	66	3	19	5	31	3
O'Neill	1	0	2	0				

Fall of wickets
First innings: 3, 172, 190, 266, 274, 279, 293, 302, 319, 321
Second innings: 3, 33, 66, 112, 125, 161, 186, 195, 198, 198

NSW

R. Simpson b Meckiff	95	not out 67
I. Craig lbw b Guest	80	not out 65
N. O'Neill c Jordon b Meckiff	0	
F. Misson c Crompton b Guest	21	
B. Booth c Cowper b Gaunt	7	
N. Harvey c Cowper b Guest	46	
G. Thomas b Meckiff	0	
A. Davidson c Anderson b Guest	106	
R. Benaud c Cowper b Kline	7	
J. Martin run out	0	
D. Ford not out	0	
Sundries	22	7
	384	None for 139

	O	M	R	W	O	M	R	W
Meckiff	26	4	97	3	5	1	15	0
Gaunt	10	2	37	1	2	0	16	0
Guest	22.7	0	103	4	7	0	35	0
Kline	16	1	98	1	9	0	25	0
Crompton	3	0	27	0				
Cowper					5	0	37	0
Anderson					1	0	4	0

Fall of wickets
First innings: 161, 164, 208, 212, 227, 230, 306, 325, 325, 384

NSW won by ten wickets

BOB SIMPSON

Making an astonishing comeback to captain Australia at the age of 41, nine years after quitting the first class game, Bob Simpson plays a cut shot.

BOB SIMPSON

When Bob Simpson was a boy, he used to catch flies in mid-air with either hand to amuse his schoolmates, little dreaming that such reflexes would make him an international cricket hero. He became perhaps the greatest of all slips fieldsmen, a snapper-up of unconsidered impossibilities who snared some amazing catches on the way to becoming the first Australian other than two wicketkeepers to bring off 100 catches in Test matches, taking an incredible 110 in total, plus another catch as substitute fieldsman.

Simpson was an impressionable 16-year-old when he first played for NSW, but disappointment and exile in Perth later forged him into very hard steel indeed. Acting on a Neil Harvey tip that an opening batting berth offered him better prospects than continuing to compete for a lower order Test spot, he curbed his dashing stroke-play to become a high-scoring opener and scourge of all bowlers.

Captaining Australia in 34 of his 62 Tests, which spanned a period of 21 years, Simpson hit ten centuries, scoring 4869 Test runs at an average of 46.8. In all his first class matches, he posted 60 centuries with a personal best of 359 for NSW against Queensland in 1963–64.

His run crawl for 12 hours 42 minutes to reach 311 against England at Old Trafford in 1964 remained the highest knock by any man captaining his country until Graham Gooch's 333 against India at Lord's in 1990, and remains the longest innings played by an Australian in Test cricket.

This mammoth innings in his 30th Test ended Simpson's long and puzzling struggle for his first Test century. After being dismissed in the 90s for the third time, he had predicted: 'It'll come, and when it does I'll make it a double.' Prophetic words indeed. He followed up with 201 against the West Indies in Bridgetown, Barbados, in 1965, then 225 against England in Adelaide in 1965–66.

Simpson joined forces with Bill Lawry to form the most productive of all Australian opening pairs. Their record 382 partnership against the West Indies in Barbados in 1965 surpassed their 244 in Adelaide against England in 1965–66 and 201 at Old Trafford in 1964.

Apart from his batting and catching, Simpson bowled slow leg spinners well enough to take 71 Test wickets, with the stupendous Gary Sobers admitting that he found difficulty in picking the Australian's googly. He bade farewell to Test cricket for the first time a few days before turning 32 by snaring five Indian wickets in Sydney.

It has been suggested that Simpson, now coach of the Australian Test team, has returned more often to centre stage than Dame Nellie Melba. At the age of 41, nine years after he had quit the first class game, he made the most astonishing comeback in Australian cricket history to lead a team of raw recruits in a series against India in 1977–78, after Kerry Packer's cataclysmic disruption of world cricket had ripped the heart out of the Australian side. Originally Simpson had been the man Packer wanted to run World Series Cricket.

It was a thrilling series, with Australia winning 3–2 and Simpson cleverly deflecting and placing the ball to hit scores of 176 and 100 as he headed the batting aggregate with 539 at an average of 53.9, a truly phenomenal performance. He turned 42 during the fifth Test in Adelaide and then took the Australian team to the West Indies.

Robert Baddeley Simpson was born in the inner Sydney suburb of Marrickville on 3 February 1936, the youngest of three sons of a soccer-playing printer who migrated from Falkirk in Scotland. He practised cricket so frequently with brothers Bill and Jack on an old tennis court that he was batting stylishly for NSW a week before turning 17.

After being overlooked for successive Australian tours to the West Indies and England, Simpson at 20 decided to move to Perth where he would be a big fish in a small pond. The chance of batting twice in most matches when playing for weaker Western Australia would give him an opportunity to stake an undeniable claim for a Test cap.

The upshot was an Australian tour to South Africa in 1957–58 when Simpson played five Tests but was dissatisfied with his batting, in spite of a couple of centuries outside the Test arena. He took note of a Neil Harvey tip to become more side-on, especially in back-foot defence.

After a lone Test innings against the 1958–59 English team in which a nick on to his pad went undetected, Simpson was dropped. He promptly took himself off to Accrington in the Lancashire League to reshape his technique at Harvey's urging, in preparation for his new role as an opening bat. Simpson explains:

> It was good advice from Neil Harvey because I wasn't going to stay in the Australian side batting down the list. I was always terribly naturally gifted and balanced and Harvey saw this.
>
> It took me two years to change styles. I tightened up and eliminated certain strokes. Big drives early in the innings. Hooking was out, too, and I was a big hooker in the early days. I computerised my game by getting rid of the risky shots. I became more aware of singles and rotating the strike. Trying not to let the same bowler have more than two or three balls in a row at you.

Going in first for Western Australia, Simpson schooled himself to bat on and on as he achieved instant success: 98, 236 not out and 230 not out in the first three games. Over two consecutive matches he was on view eight days for every ball as a batsman, bowler and fielder, and at one stage his thirst for runs produced a batting average of 300. He had indeed eliminated the shots likely to get him into trouble.

Returning to the Australian side for the 1960–61 series against the West Indies, Simpson defied the body-crunchers of the world's swiftest bowler, Wesley Hall, to notch 92 in his comeback innings and finish the series with 445 runs at an average of almost 50. In his last innings of the rubber, Simpson took to Hall and slashed 18 off his opening over.

On Australia's subsequent tour of England in 1961, Simpson moved up the order to open the batting with left-hander Bill Lawry for the first time in the fourth Test at Old Trafford. Their second innings partnership of 113 set the stage for Richie Benaud to snatch an amazing victory by taking 6 for 70. It was a pairing that would figure in some monumental stands.

By appointing Simpson vice-captain to Benaud in 1963, the NSW selectors gave more than a hint of who was to be the next Australian captain. In his first game as Richie's lieutenant, Simpson showed the killer touch by piling up 359 to lift NSW to 661 in reply to Queensland's 613 in Brisbane. On New Year's Day 1964, he took over from Benaud as Australian captain midway through a series with the touring South Africans.

With a team derided by the critics, Simpson and Co. retained the Ashes 1–0 in England; on the way home he hit 153 and 115 against Pakistan in Karachi. With morale nose-diving, Simpson then led unsuccessful tours to the West Indies and South Africa before stepping down to give the Australian captaincy to Bill Lawry midway through a 1967–68 home series with India in which he posted 103 and 109 in consecutive Tests.

Oddly enough, Simpson doesn't plump for his series-clinching 311 against England as his greatest innings, nominating instead his classic if slow 225 against England in Adelaide in the 1965–66 series. Not even a gastric attack could interrupt him. Unable to keep down breakfast or lunch on the second day of his innings, Simpson had doses of physic sent out at the drinks intervals. He was seventh out at 480 and that night could nibble on nothing more than a chicken leg. Eventually Australia reached 516 in reply to England's 241 and bowled them out for 266 and an innings victory which squared the rubber. Simpson recalls:

I'd missed the first Test with a broken wrist and the third Test in Sydney with chicken pox, and with two Tests to go we were one down in the series.

The selectors had dropped Graham McKenzie, choosing Peter Allan, but when Allan was injured Garth came back and took six wickets to bowl England out for less than 250. Bill Lawry and I began Australia's innings early on the Saturday and broke up the English bowlers by pushing them around for singles. We chipped and ran from ball one. Soon the English players were abusing each other as they unsuccessfully tried to stop us getting the singles. When Bill was finally out for 119, we'd figured in a record opening partnership against England of 244. I rate my innings so highly because it helped lift us from one down to square the series and thus retain the Ashes.

Looking at the Simpson–Lawry partnership which rewrote the record books, Simpson says:

I think it's absolutely essential to have a right- and left-hander opening the innings. That's why we were so anxious to get Mark Taylor into the Australian side. It unbalances the opposing attack to have a right- and left-hander circulating the strike, pushing the singles. I was lifted up the order to take Colin McDonald's place as Bill's opening partner in the Old Trafford Test against England in 1961. We were both good manoeuvrers of the ball, with the ability to change the pace of shots, so we were able to pick up those crucial singles and rotate the strike. Although Bill and I were good friends, we never spent much time together off the field. We had totally different interests; I was very keen to play golf on tour, but Bill wasn't a golfer. He was interested in pigeons.

By the time the Australians got to Old Trafford for the fourth Test against England in 1964, Simpson's failure to score a Test century had become one of cricket's biggest talking points. After the first two Tests were drawn, Peter Burge smashed 160 at Leeds to give Ashes holder, Australia, a 1–0 lead in the series. Now it was time to grind England into the dust. Simpson recalls:

We had been rated the worst side ever to leave Australia. Sound familiar? Still, it was super motivation. We won the toss and chose to bat, and the wicket turned out to be quite lively. Bill and I really had to struggle to get through the lunch. In fact, one of the umpires told me at the end of the day that if I'd put England in to bat, we'd have bowled them out for under 200. We had a very good trio of medium-pacers in Graham McKenzie, Neil Hawke and Grahame Corling.

With an old-style display of ruthless Test batting, Simpson and Lawry put together 201 to eclipse the old opening record against England of 180 set by Warren Bardsley and Syd Gregory in 1909. Shrugging off the balls that beat the bat, they took no chances and played no risky strokes, although Lawry struck three sixes before being run out for 106. At the end of the day Australia was 2 for 253. Simpson reached his first century in 30 Tests with a tickle to fine-leg off bat and pad, and at the close was talking of a first innings total of 650.

The second day was a slow, grinding war of attrition after which the scoreboard towered over England's hopes like a tombstone — Australia 4 for 570 with Simpson still there with 265. The eighth double century of Simpson's career made his previous failure to score a Test century all the more puzzling. Denis Compton, the former champion English batsman, noted:

> Bobby Simpson is still there after 12 hours of batting; that was a credit to the coach who taught him his defensive strokes. Unfortunately a different man must have taught him his attacking strokes because we didn't see so many of those.
>
> The main qualities of this innings were application and concentration. Over the years I have heard Australians in their thousands bewail the slowness of Sir Leonard Hutton at taking 13 hours in scoring 364 runs in 1938. Yet here was Simpson, still 99 short of that figure, having batted just over an hour less.
>
> The purpose of the operation was simple and obviously Simpson was going to build such a score that there was no possibility of his losing the match or the Ashes and so that any deterioration in the weather or the pitch must be in his favour. I admired the size of the innings, but I must repeat that I thought it criminal that a player with such a range of shots should have stifled them for so long. There are not enough players so talented that the game can afford that.

From the first ball of the third day, Simpson went after the bowling like a bull terrier sprung from a leash. He went down the wicket and straight drove off spinner John Mortimore for six and slashed at almost every ball before swinging his bat like a sledgehammer at fast man John Price and touching a catch to wicketkeeper Jim Parks. He had scored 311 out of 652 runs in a stay of 762 minutes which produced a six and 23 fours. It was a massive effort in which he played for his side from the very first ball. He could well have knuckled down and gone for Sir Gary Sobers' world Test record of 365, but he spurned the temptation. With Ken

Barrington posting 256, England got 611 in reply to Australia's 656 and the Ashes were safely in Australia's keeping.

When Simpson and Lawry again joined forces in the West Indies in 1965, they came up against Charlie Griffith, a cheat who wilfully threw a cricket ball instead of bowling it. With Wesley Hall firing down his thunderballs from the other end, the Australians were faced with bowling of savage intent. Many of the team became obsessed with the menace of Griffith's bouncers and yorkers. With the home crowd baying for blood, Griffith was allowed to subject Simpson to five bouncers in six balls before an umpire warned him for intimidatory bowling. Simpson's understandable resentment of Griffith's unpenalised bent-arm action caused a bitter walking-off outburst to Sir Frank Worrell: 'How will that go down in the score-book — chucked out?' Simpson recalls:

> Griffith chucked alright and was as lethal as any bowler I've faced. Even Tony Cozier [the West Indian commentator] admitted his bent-arm made him dangerous. Somebody in Sydney sent us some helmets, but we didn't feel we needed them. Bill Lawry got hit in the Barbados Test, but the ball was deflected from his shoulder. We ran into a lot of bouncers from Hall and Griffith from day one. We lost the first two Tests, but by the fourth Test in Barbados, we were getting accustomed to the pace.

In the Barbados Test, Simpson won the toss and with Lawry had to survive a devilish opening spell from Hall and Griffith in which Lawry was hit on the head and Griffith was warned for intimidatory bowling to Simpson. After the first hour, the Australians took control and produced some merciless batting on a perfect pitch. On and on they sailed, and at the close were none for 263, a sensational and totally unexpected start, with Lawry hitting three sixes. The next day he and Simpson carried on to have a good chance of breaking the world record opening partnership of 413 held by India's Mankad and Roy until Simpson inside-edged Hall on to his stumps to be out for 201 with the score at 382. He had played some glorious strokes.

The surprising thing about Simpson's prowess as a slips fieldsman is that he was put there on the whim of skipper Keith Miller when he took the field as substitute for NSW when only 17. Running out to deputise for a player who had left the field in a game against Victoria at the SCG, Simpson asked, 'Where do you want me?' Miller seemed a little puzzled but then nonchalantly pointed to the slips and said, 'Go there.' It was not the acceptable thing for a substitute to field in such a key catching position, but that didn't worry Miller. Previously Simpson had fielded on the boundary, but within half an hour he had caught Neil Harvey and Harry Lambert. He stayed in the slips ever since.

As the coach of Australia's Test team and cricket manager of the Leicestershire county club in England, Simpson is in a unique position to compare today's players with the greats of the 1950s, '60s and '70s. He speaks with typical candour:

> People say today's players are fitter and field better, but I won't buy that. Don't try to tell me that today's Australian team fields any better than the 1961 team when we had Neil Harvey, Alan Davidson and Norm O'Neill [Simpson modestly omits himself]. Today's players are no better than the guys of ten, 20 and 30 years ago. They don't think any better. After NSW won the Sheffield Shield in 1989–90, Geoff Lawson said it was the best NSW team ever. Well, we won the Shield nine years in a row with as many as ten Test players in the team. Lawson's team has a fair bit to do yet.
>
> As a coach, I'm generally very sympathetic with batting and bowling because I know the pitfalls, but I get totally annoyed with fielding lapses due to poor concentration. I'm a good watcher of cricket, and that's something that frustrates me about the modern game. Guys say they can't watch the game.
>
> I'm not a hard person. I'm demanding of the players, but I don't demand from them any more than what their talents indicate they should be giving. Even when you reach the Test level, you've still got a fair amount to learn.
>
> There isn't as much sledging now as there was in the '70s when you had guys at short leg and gully mouthing off with all sorts of nonsense. In my day, we had little verbal discussion, with little more than Freddie Trueman disputing the legality of your parents' marriage.
>
> The selectors didn't speak a lot to the players in the old days. Now they speak a lot and I'm not sure if that's a good or a bad thing. Kids these days are taught to query things, so when I'm coaching I can't just tell a guy to do something, I've got to explain why. Then everybody's happy.

When not coaching Australia or managing Leicestershire, Simpson is a doting grandfather who runs Bob Simpson Promotions, which (among other things) markets artificial grass. He remains optimistic that somewhere, be it in the bush or an urban ghetto, a prodigy is waiting to emerge.

AUSTRALIA v ENGLAND
Adelaide, 28 January–1 February 1965–66

England

G. Boycott c Chappell b Hawke	22	lbw b McKenzie	12
R.W. Barber b McKenzie	0	c Grout b Hawke	19
J.H. Edrich c Simpson b Mckenzie	5	c Simpson b Hawke	1
K.F. Barrington lbw b Walters	60	c Chappell b Hawke	102
M.C. Cowdrey run out	38	c Grout b Stackpole	35
M.J.K. Smith b Veivers	29	c McKenzie b Stackpole	5
J.M. Parks c Stackpole b McKenzie	49	run out	16
F.J. Titmus lbw b McKenzie	33	c Grout b Hawke	53
D.A. Allen c Simpson b McKenzie	2	not out	5
D.J. Brown c Thomas b McKenzie	1	c & b Hawke	0
I.J. Jones not out	0	c Lawry b Veivers	8
Sundries	2		10
	241		266

	O	M	R	W	O	M	R	W
McKenzie	21.7	4	48	6	18	4	53	1
Hawke	23	2	69	1	21	6	54	5
Walters	14	0	50	1	9	0	47	0
Stackpole	5	0	30	0	14	3	33	2
Chappell	4	1	18	0	22	4	53	0
Veivers	13	3	24	1	3.7	0	16	1

Fall of wickets
First innings: 7, 25, 33, 105, 178, 210, 212, 222, 241
Second innings: 23, 31, 32, 114, 123, 163, 244, 253, 257, 266

Australia

R.B. Simpson b Titmus b Jones	225
W.M. Lawry b Titmus	119
G. Thomas b Jones	52
T.R. Veivers c Parks b Jones	1
P.J. Burge c Parks b Jones	27
K.D. Walters c Parks b Brown	0
I.M. Chappell c Edrich b Jones	17
K.R. Stackpole c Parks b Jones	43
N.J.N. Hawke not out	20
A.T.W. Grout b Titmus	4
G.D. McKenzie lbw b Titmus	1
Sundries	7
	516

	O	M	R	W
Jones	29	3	118	6
Brown	28	4	109	1
Boycott	7	3	33	0
Titmus	37	6	116	3
Allen	21	1	103	0
Barber	4	0	30	0

Fall of wickets: 244, 331, 333, 379, 383, 415, 480, 501, 506, 516

Australia won by an innings and 9 runs

DOUG WALTERS

The style of Doug Walters, who hooked the day's last ball for six to complete a Test century in a session against England.

DOUG WALTERS

With practically unrazored cheeks, Doug Walters was awarded an Australian cap at 19. He promptly scored 155 against England in his first Test innings at the Woolangabba ground set amid Brisbane's fig and poinsettia trees.

His first scoring stroke in the Test arena that damp day in November 1965 was a rocketing straight drive for four off the second ball he received from off spinner Fred Titmus. When the tyro from Marshdale up in the sticks near Dungog, NSW, got 115 in the next Test in Melbourne, he became the first batsman since Bill Ponsford in 1924–25 to announce himself to an unsuspecting cricket world with centuries in his first two Tests.

With rare dash and daring, unconventional genius Walters proceeded to whip up some of the game's most dazzling centuries, twice scoring a Test 100 in a session. To achieve this feat in Perth in 1974, he joyfully hooked a six off the day's last ball from England's fast man Bob Willis.

On another occasion in 1969 Walters savaged a West Indian attack including Wes Hall, Charlie Griffith, Gary Sobers and Lance Gibbs to score 242 and 103 at the Sydney Cricket Ground, thus becoming the first player to hit up a double century and a century in the same Test. All this while suffering from a back injury sustained when he slipped as he put the garbage bin out in the rain.

You don't expect Test cricketers to get hurt like that, but the big thing about this patently decent fellow is that everybody can identify with him in one way or another. Kids lined up to climb on Uncle Doug or get his autograph. The cricket fans relished his dashing strokes, while the yobbos on the SCG Hill like a bloke who they know loves a beer as much as they do.

A laconic, unpretentious and uncomplicated soul, Walters indeed relishes a drop of what tennis hero John Newcombe calls the tasty brown stuff. He once quaffed 44 cans of beer on a flight from Sydney to London with the Australian cricket team. Silly, but he did it.

And if there was a poker school in the dressing room, Walters would be in the middle of it, invariably puffing away on a cigarette as he squinted at his cards like a man riding shotgun on a stagecoach.

In his foreword to Doug's book *One for the Road*, Ian Chappell explains why Walters was a vital if inconsistent part of the Australian cricket war machine:

> During my term as captain of Australia, I often said I wouldn't want to tour without Doug Walters. Apart from exceptional skill as a batsman, his sneaky little medium-pacers that regularly broke partnerships and his brilliance in the field, he had the capacity to keep the team loose off the field as well as on it. Doug's sense of humour and his delight in pulling off practical jokes was a big thing in lifting the mood and morale of the team.

Knowing off spinner Ashley Mallett had a fear of spiders, Walters bought a toy one and, during a Test match, stuck it to the ball with a piece of chewing gum then tossed it to the unsuspecting South Australian. The crowd was puzzled when Mallett suddenly hurled the ball into the outfield like an unpinned grenade.

Walters also could be relied upon to come up with an hilarious remark which would have his team-mates in stitches at exactly the right moment. When skipper Greg Chappell ordered brother Trevor to roll up a last-ball underarm grubber to give Australia a six-run victory over New Zealand in a one-day match in Melbourne in 1981, the players sat in stunned silence when they got back to the dressing room.

Then Walters piped up: 'Well, Greg, you've just destroyed my faith in one of the great stories of cricket. I always thought a game was never over until the last ball was bowled — but I haven't seen it yet.' Laughter all around.

In the 1974 Test against England in Brisbane, tail-ender Derek Underwood's stubborn straight bat was defying the fireballs of Jeff Thomson and Dennis Lillee and Max Walker's nagging deliveries. The Australians were desperate for a wicket. Walters was brought into the attack and his first ball was the gentlest of half-volleys that slipped from his hand. Having faced the blinding pace of Thompson and Lillee, Underwood hit too early and lobbed the simplest of catches to Ian Redpath in the covers.

When the Australian players rushed to congratulate the man known as the Golden Arm for his ability as a partnership-splitter, Walters held up his hand. 'No, no,' he said, 'Don't give me all the credit. Give some to Derek. A lesser batsman wouldn't have got a bat to it.'

You're supposed to take the bat back in a straight line, but Walters lifted his towards third slip, a flaw that made him vulnerable against the seaming and swinging ball in England where he failed to score a Test century in four tours. He could be a nervous starter, too.

When dropped from the fifth Test at The Oval in 1972, Doug's character shone through. Though his heart must have been sinking, he play-acted to the tour selectors in the interests of team spirit: 'Beauty, I won't have to be up early for nets.'

Walters was a marvellous improviser with the eye of a kestrel and was always willing to give the ball a crack in scoring 5357 Test runs at 48.26 per innings. He was particularly strong on the leg side and scored a host of runs with superb strokes through mid-wicket.

England skipper Ray Illingworth rated him the best outfielder in the world. Walters, with 49 Test wickets in his portfolio, was a very useful third seamer who could move the ball both ways and came at the batsman much quicker than expected.

Kevin Douglas Walters (born 21 December 1945) began with the simple joys of bush cricket. The mats, the malthoid, the cracked concrete pitches. Men and boys playing under azure skies with the heat too much for all but the players and the flies. With the batting side sitting under gaunt gumtrees, the sound of Test match commentary or horse racing blares out from a portable radio.

Magpies and kookaburras could well have been the only other spectators when a kid called Doug Walters rushed through helping to milk the cows on the family dairy farm and headed for a hit with the local Police Boys Club team on a Saturday morning. It was virtually the same start for other bush boys Don Bradman, Bill O'Reilly, Stan McCabe, Alan Davidson and Mark Taylor, all of whom went on to win world cricketing fame.

Guided unobtrusively by his father Ted, young Doug played cricket on the verandah and later on a pitch rolled out of antbed. While still in short pants, he was a prodigious wicket-taker for the Police Boys team, chalking up such outrageous figures as 9 for 8, 9 for 4 and 8 for 7.

At 17, Walters was whisked into the NSW team to play a Queensland team boosted by the sizzling bowling of Wes Hall, the West Indian star. He made 50 in the second innings, believing to this day that Hall generously refrained from bowling him a bouncer. The following season Walters announced to the cricketing world that he was something special by single-handedly destroying South Australia in Adelaide with 253 and 7 for 63.

Walters was totally calm, totally mature and totally in command of his destiny in scoring 155 in the first Test of the 1965–66 series against Mike Smith's Englishmen when just short of his 20th birthday. Marshdale's entire population of 112 was glued to TV sets and radios during an unforgettable 48 minutes as Doug edged through 90s in which there was an interruption for drinks, another break when a runaway dog took the field, a near run-out at 98 and remorselessly tight bowling by Fred Titmus and David Allen throughout. With his father Ted forced to stay home after suffering a heart attack, Walters raised his bat to the ovation that greeted his hundred and said to himself, 'This one's for you, dad.'

Back in Marshdale Bill Hudson lost 100 schooners of beer when he rashly bet that Doug wouldn't make a Test century first time out against the Englishmen.

In his book, *The Doug Walters Story*, Walters recalls:

> Getting selected for Australia was the biggest thrill of my life. Those schoolboy dreams of playing for my country had come true. To make 155 in the first innings was simply a bonus. It was unbelievable.
>
> My dad and I were driving home to Dungog after I'd made a century for NSW against the Poms when the team was announced on the radio. It was outside the Darlinghurst Post Office just up from Taylor Square. Dad and I just looked at each other just choked with emotion. Not a word passed between us.
>
> I didn't drink in those days, but I wish now I could have stopped the old Mini and had a beer with dad, who died not long afterwards. He loved his beer, but he celebrated with me with a cup of tea.

Two years later, as 2783873 Private Walters, K.D., he averaged 127 in two Tests against the touring Indians and notched his 1000th Test run in only his 11th Test on the 1968 tour of England. Then he came home to pile up 699 runs (average 116.5) against the West Indies, climaxing the rubber with 242 and 103 in Sydney.

But as far as centuries go, Walters got his biggest buzz from avenging four tours of England without a Test century by carving 100 runs in a session from Mike Denness' touring Englishmen in Perth in 1974.

Sent in to bat, England collapsed from 1 for 99 to 208 all out on the opening day and when Greg Chappell was out for 62 just before tea on the second afternoon, Australia was nicely poised at 4 for 192.

Walters recalls:

> After I'd batted for a couple of overs to be 3 not out at the tea break, Greg Chappell said he'd paved the way for me to get 100 in the last session.
>
> It was one of those magic days when the ball seemed to hit the middle of the bat, so I went for my shots. When I was 67 at drinks I thought I'd make Greg's prediction come true rather easily. In fact, I seemed set to be about 130 at stumps.

Ross Edwards was my partner, and although he did his damnedest to give me the strike, at one stage I didn't face a ball for four or five overs. I was on 93 when Bob Willis began the last over, and with Ross taking strike that century in a session seemed to have gone out the gate. He got a single off the first ball, which left me with seven balls to pick up those ten runs.

When Willis pitched his first ball to me short, it caught the top edge when I attempted to hook and flew over wicketkeeper Alan Knott into the sight screen on the second bounce. It was a miscue, but I was happy to take it.

I figured I'd get another short ball or two in the six balls remaining because Willis had been averaging two or three bouncers an over to me. I was on the back foot waiting, but balls three, four, five, six and seven were well up and pitched on the stumps.

As Willis walked back to bowl the last ball, I figured he'd dig it in short to try me out. There were two guys on the backward square leg boundary, so the bait was there to hook and risk holing out. Short it was, and I hooked. Bat and ball connected at exactly the right moment and the ball sailed over the two fieldsmen and the boundary line for six.

The crowd spilled onto the ground to slap my back after I'd taken sweet revenge for being dropped from the final Test of the last English tour. Still, this would be nothing to when the guys mobbed me in the dressing rooms.

When I walked into the room, there wasn't a soul in sight. 'Where are you, you bastards? Here is a man hitting a six off the day's last ball to complete a century in a session and you haven't got the decency to be there to hero-worship him.'

Enter Ian Chappell. 'You dopey bastard,' he exploded. 'How could you play a totally irresponsible shot like that and get out off the last ball of the day? Jesus, pal. The team comes first, not the individual.'

Chappelli glared at me for a couple of seconds — and then broke into a huge grin and hugged me as the rest of the guys came out of the showers where they'd been hiding. They had been getting back at me for a few of the little tricks I'd pulled on them.

What a reception they gave me, and they must have pulled the tops off a few too many because I was out second ball next day for 103.

The other time Walters got 100 in a session was against the West Indies at Port-of-Spain in Trinidad in 1973 when off spinner Lance Gibbs was turning the ball almost square to three short legs. He got a century between lunch and tea to finish with 112 with 16 fours and a six in a display which sent Ian Chappell and Rod Marsh into raptures. Oddly, Walters wasn't all that impressed and says, 'It's not one of my favourite innings and I don't remember that much about it. The ground has a reputation for being a difficult place to play strokes, but fortunately no one told me before I went in to bat.'

Walters has much fonder memories about his highest Test score of 250, the highest score by a number six batsman in the history of Tests, against New Zealand in Christchurch in 1976–77 when he figured in an Australian record stand of 217 for the seventh wicket with Gary Gilmour:

> I started with probably the worst 20-odd I ever scored, but after that I played as good an innings as I've ever played. The pitch was a bit dicey with some uneven bounce off not the flattest of tracks. Richard Hadlee was in their attack and the ball was seaming about quite a lot.
>
> I made the first 100 on the first day and Gus and I stayed up late to celebrate with a two-man party. The next day Gus went on to score 101 and I finished with 250, not a bad effort for a morning after the night before.

On that trip Walters became alarmed when skipper Greg Chappell introduced roadwork into the Australian team's regime. After being lapped by a stony-faced Chappell, Walters said, 'I don't want to go.' When Chappell looked at him in puzzlement, Walters said, 'I don't want to go to the Moscow Olympics.'

Recalling his stunning double of 242 and 103 against the West Indies in 1969 at the SCG, Walters claims he was extremely lucky in a couple of aspects. He claims:

> Firstly, I probably shouldn't have played. Just before the Test I was putting the garbage out at our flat. It was raining and I was wearing thongs. When I slipped and fell down 20 steps to finish lying in a crumpled heap in a pool of water, I felt I'd broken at least a couple of bones in my back.
>
> However, I'd learned my lesson after being ruled out of the first Test with nothing more than a leg strain. The Australian Cricket Board's doctor had asked me how I felt and jokingly I said I would be hard pressed to bowl 20 overs straight. He took me at my word and ruled me out, so this time I didn't even risk a precautionary X-ray.
>
> Then in the second innings Phanto [Bill Lawry] batted on much longer than most other captains would have. The match was over six days and we didn't declare until after lunch on the second last day. But there again, Phanto always did like to play it safe. The Windies brought back the old combination of Wes Hall and Charlie Griffith and on the first morning of the match came word that both guys had been left out of the team to tour England. As a result they produced some of the fastest bowling I have ever faced.
>
> Charlie had had a suspect action which he changed after our 1965 tour of

> the West Indies, but he reverted to his old whippy action in the second innings. I'm not saying he threw, but he was far quicker than at any other time on tour.
>
> I remember one ball in particular as it was the most lethal I ever faced. It reared from just short of a good length and although I nearly doubled over backwards trying to get out of the way, it grazed my forehead on the way through. And those were the days before helmets.

Doug Walters' services to Australian cricket have been recognised in a variety of ways. There is the Doug Walters Stand at the Sydney Cricket Ground, to remind new generations of fans of his efforts, while the NSW Cricket Association staged a benefit year for Walters — the first time this had been done. Walters, now a father of four, is contentedly in retirement, though he is kept busy with promotional work, coaching kids and the odd spot of TV cricket commentary. His TV commercials with Max Walker for Toohey's are absolute classics.

AUSTRALIA v ENGLAND
Perth, 13–17 December 1974

England

D. Lloyd c G. Chappell b Thomson	49	c G. Chappell b Walker	35
B.W. Luckhurst c Mallett b Walker	27	c Mallett b Lillee	23
M.C. Cowdrey b Thomson	22	lbw b Thomson	41
A.W. Greig c Mallett b Walker	23	c G. Chappell b Thomson	32
K.W.R. Fletcher c Redpath b Lillee	4	c Marsh b Thomson	0
M.H. Denness c G. Chappell b Lillee	2	c Redpath b Thomson	20
A.P.E. Knott c Redpath b Walters	51	c G. Chappell b Lillee	18
F.J. Titmus c Redpath b Walters	10	c G. Chappell b Mallett	61
C.M. Old c G. Chappell b I. Chappell	7	c Thomson b Mallett	43
G.G. Arnold run out	1	c Mallett b Thomson	4
R.G.D. Willis not out	4	not out	0
Sundries	8		16
	208		293

	O	M	R	W	O	M	R	W
Lillee	16	4	48	2	22	5	59	2
Thomson	15	6	45	2	25	4	93	5
Walker	20	5	49	2	24	7	76	1
Mallett	10	3	35	0	11.1	4	32	2
Walters	2.3	0	13	2	9	0	17	0
I. Chappell	2	0	10	1				

Fall of wickets
First innings: 44, 99, 119, 128, 132, 132, 194, 201, 202, 208
Second innings: 62, 106, 124, 124, 154, 156, 219, 285, 293, 293

Australia

I.R. Redpath st Knott b Titmus	41	not out	12
W.J. Edwards c Lloyd b Greig	30	lbw b Arnold	0
I.M. Chappell c Knott b Arnold	25	not out	
G.S. Chappell c Greig b Willis	62		
R. Edwards b Arnold	115		
K.D. Walters c Fletcher b Willis	103		
R.W. Marsh c Lloyd b Titmus	41		
M.H.N. Walker c Knott b Old	19		
D.K. Lillee b Old	11		
A.A. Mallett c Knott b Old	0		
J.R. Thomson not out	11		
Sundries	23		
	481		1 for 23

	O	M	R	W	O	M	R	W
Willis	22	0	91	2	2	0	8	0
Arnold	27	1	129	2	1.7	0	15	1
Old	22.6	3	85	3				
Greig	9	0	69	1				
Titmus	28	3	84	2				

Fall of wickets
First innings: 64, 101, 113, 192, 362, 416, 449, 462, 481
Second innings: 4

Australia won by 9 wickets

IAN CHAPPELL

Both as batsman and as captain, Ian Chappell has earned his place amongst Australia's sporting heroes.

IAN CHAPPELL

'Lillee and Thomson, the Chappells and Co., white flannelled undertakers happy you should go.' John Snow, English cricketer

Fidgeting, gum-chewing and combative, Ian Chappell was a batsman with guts and belligerence, while as a captain he is right up there with Sir Donald Bradman and Richie Benaud.

Watching him facing up to the fireballs of the West Indian fast bowlers was like watching some unexpectedly tough little kid walking up to the school bully and kicking him smartly in the shins. His super-confident batting was marked by booming drives through a wide sector and hooked missiles that either flew to the boundary or into long leg's hands.

With superb footwork, Chappell posted 14 centuries in his 5345 runs at an average of 42.42 in 75 Tests, captaining Australia in 30 of them and never losing a series. He won 15 Tests as skipper and lost only five. Bowling his leg breaks all too infrequently, Ian took 20 Test wickets and was a tremendous first slip who snapped up 103 catches, an Australian record until brother Greg broke it.

Many keen judges say that Chappell, on all types of wickets, was the best batsman in the world during his Test career. He had wonderful success in the most difficult spot in the order — number three. If Earth had to pick one man to play an innings for the planet on an unknown wicket somewhere else in the Universe, Chappell would have been the choice of his peers.

He and brothers Greg (his successor as Australian captain) and Trevor have cricket in their chromosomes, as through their mother Jeanne they are grandsons of Vic Richardson, who captained Australia in the 1930s.

As batsman, Ian and Greg are different types, as different as they are in personality. Greg is the elegant stroke-player of the pair, with Ian the more rugged and ebullient in his shotmaking. In Wellington, New Zealand, in 1973–74, Greg scored 247 not out and 133, while Ian got 145 and 121, the only instance of brothers posting a century in each innings of the same Test.

As Australian and South Australian captain, straight-shooter Ian figured in a series of stormy skirmishes with the cricket establishment, making it forcefully clear that in his eyes at least, the players must come first. Expletives were never deleted and sometimes Chappell went over the top, but his players would do anything for him. Harking to accusations of

Pommie-bashing, English skipper Mike Brearley declared, 'Playing against a team with Ian Chappell as captain turns a cricket match into gang warfare.'

Chappell says:

> I've got past the point of caring about being labelled controversial. I mean, I'm honest and say what I think. So if the truth is controversial, then sure, I'm controversial. I've never seen telling the truth as controversial. I was brought up to do that.
>
> If the guys gave me their full support on the field, I had to give them my complete support off it. I'm not for one minute saying I wouldn't have locked horns with the Australian Cricket Board anyhow. I would have because I'm an impatient man. I don't suffer fools. If I see some stupid thing that's wrong and can mean the difference between the Australian cricket team winning and losing, I want it fixed NOW. I don't want to play games. I want the problem solved straight away.
>
> All this talk about me sledging is bullshit. Believe it or not, I was quiet on the field, with most instruction being given through hand signals. But if a quick bowler or somebody had a go at me, I'd have a go back. With my baseball background as a catcher, I liked all the back and forth stuff.

Of course Chappell upset people. But that was his strength, this confrontationist attitude. It endeared him to the Australian team which he nurtured to become the world's number one with the thunderbolts of Dennis Lillee and Jeff Thomson.

Chappell's critics downgrade his captaincy with the churlish, 'Yes, but what about the champions he had like Lillee and Thommo and brother Greg?' Instead they should assess the 2–0 series win in the West Indies in 1973 when Ian brilliantly used a second-string attack headed by Max Walker and Jeff Hammond. There was no Lillee, Thomson or Bob Massie in those Tests. And didn't Bradman and Benaud have some great players too?

Those who played alongside Chappell will remember him not for punching a Guyanese official, nor for cursing an umpire, nor for dropping his trousers at the Adelaide Oval with his backside bared to the committee box. They saw him as a firm, skilled, experienced, tough fighter. An uncompromising winner. A man who understood players, their moods and their problems.

For Chappell's favourite century, we go to The Oval for the fifth Test of the 1971 series when Australia, down 2–1, could no longer win the Ashes. Crammed with action, the final Test attracted such crowds that the gates were shut on full houses three days running. Chappell recalls:

The game before the Test was at Northampton, where they had a bloody awful track. To make any runs you'd have to concentrate like mad, and as I was feeling a bit stuffed and the Test was so close I wasn't in the mood. I made a wild swing and was bowled for five.

When I got back to the dressing room, I saw my dad Martin and Jeanne sitting in the stand. I had a couple of miniature bats Martin wanted autographed, so I took them down.

He greeted me with, 'That was a bloody awful shot.'

'Get stuffed, Martin,' I said, 'I've got a Test match next week and I wasn't going to waste any concentration out there.'

In the Test, we bowled England out for 284. Greg and I were in pretty quickly just as we'd been at Lord's when Greg got his 131, the dig he always says is the best he ever played. That time they were trying to bounce me out and I got away to a quick start which left Greg behind. When I got out for 50-odd, Greg just took over and got his 100.

The same thing happened at The Oval where Graeme Watson and Keith Stackpole were out early to make us two for bugger-all. Greg and I got together and it was pretty hard work. This time they were just trying to maintain good line and length instead of trying to bounce me. John Snow was bowling pretty well and there was a bit of bounce in the track. In fact, it probably was the best cricket wicket I've ever played on in England.

Greg and I went along quietly but steadily and hit the 50 mark about the same time. Then he got away from me and I was in the late 80s when he reached his 100.

I was conscious that I'd had a pretty average sort of tour, getting 50s in the Tests at Lord's and Trent Bridge but not going on with it. Greg was in much better form than me, so I just made sure I stayed in and let him have as much strike as possible. I wasn't going to try to stay with him and get myself out.

We never used to talk at all when batting, and when Greg got his 100 I just went down and said, 'Well played.' He promptly lofted a ball from Ray Illingworth wide of mid-on, and thinking he had lost his concentration I was down the wicket like a shot. 'Come on,' I said, 'we've got a long way to go.' Greg replied, 'Don't worry, it's alright.'

Greg always was prepared to loft the ball more than me. Some of my hook shots went in the air, but they weren't necessarily meant to go there. In front of the wicket I always tried to keep the ball down because I didn't fancy myself as being much of a dobber. Greg was very good at picking the ball up off his pads and hitting it over the infield, particularly off the quicker bowlers.

When Greg was out for 113, we'd put together 201 — our first three-figure partnership together and made even better by having Martin, Jeanne and brother Trevor sitting in the stand. It's a funny thing, but even though I batted three and Greg four for South Australia, as soon as we came together one of us would get out. Our 80-odd at Lord's was the first time we'd fired as a pair.

However, this was just the start because we subsequently had some big ones. We made cricket history by each getting a century in both innings in a Test against New Zealand in 1974 and we had a 300 partnership in Barbados. We had a couple of big partnerships in the Tests in the West Indies, too.

I remember bringing up my 100 after Illy [Ray Illingworth] had taken the slip out and I came down the track to hit him through the covers. The ball drifted away a bit and I nicked it. By the time I looked around it was well gone, so I'm not sure if it went in the air or along the ground. Still, no matter. I knew there wasn't a slip and it went for four.

The only other shot I recall is the one I got out to for 118; Geoff Arnold surprised me with a bouncer and I mishooked it to Snowy [John Snow] at fine leg. I wasn't really expecting a bouncer from Arnold, and I was getting a bit tired.

Apart from the Chappells and my team-mates, the happiest man at The Oval was Ted Dexter, the former English captain who'd been to the Ladbrokes tent and put 200 quid on Greg and I to make 100s at odds of 12–1. Ted had taken a look at the wicket, checked the weather forecast and made up his mind that somebody was going to make a century. Greg was the form player, but his odds of 3–1 didn't appeal. Then Ted saw 12–1 about the two of us and took it. Why me? I'd only made a couple of 50s in the series. 'Well, Chappelli,' he said, 'You were due.'

When I came out of the dressing room, there was Mum, who'd obviously had a few gins to celebrate. She threw her arms around me and said, 'You were right what you said to Dad about saving up your concentration.' Martin shook my hand and said, 'Well done,' but I think he was a bit upset with Jeanne for taking my side.

I was too stuffed to go out and celebrate, but Trevor made it a family treble by hitting a century in a club match that weekend. Ladbrokes presented Greg and I with gold cufflinks, mine engraved with IC 118 and his with GC 113. What made that century so special was that it helped us square the series and turn the corner as a team.

After that Test was over, Chappell went down to the Gray Nicolls factory to pick up a few bats to take home. At that stage he was using a bat weighing 2lb 4oz or 2lb 5oz. After choosing his bats, John Newbury, who was in charge, asked Ian to try another. He took a swing and said, 'Jeez that's well balanced. It's got a beautiful feeling.'

'Do you know how heavy it is?' John asked.

Chappell had a sneaking suspicion it was a bit heavier than the bats he usually used because there was a lot of wood in it, but was astounded to discover it was 2lb 10oz. He promptly asked whose bat it was.

'I've made it up for your brother Greg,' Newbury said. 'He specifically asked to try a 2lb 10oz.'

'Well, he's had bad luck,' Chappell said. 'I've got my hands on it and possession is nine-tenths of the law.' When Newbury protested, Ian added, 'Well, he's my brother. I'll explain it to him. You'd better make him up another 2lb 10oz, hadn't you?' Chappell continues:

> I took the bat back to London that night and naturally didn't say anything to Greg. On the way home, Greg and I stopped over in South Africa for double wicket competitions in Salisbury and Johannesburg. First up in Salisbury, we played Tony Greig and Basil d'Oliveira. They got a pile of runs, 80-odd off eight overs, so we had a job on our hands.
>
> Greggy was bowling and bang! I lofted a ball and it's gone way down the ground for six. As they got the ball from the back of the pavilion, Greg came down and said, 'Jesus, that's a good bat you've got.'
>
> 'I'll tell you a story about it after this innings,' I said. We got the runs and Greg said, 'Give me a feel of that bat.' He picked it up. 'Gee, it feels nice.'
>
> 'Well, yeah,' I said and when I told him the story, Greg wasn't too happy.
>
> 'That's my bloody bat,' he said.
>
> 'Bullshit, mate,' I replied. 'You've got no chance of getting it back.'
>
> That bat lasted me right through the series at home against Pakistan in which I got 196 in Adelaide. By the time I took it to the West Indies in 1973 I was putting fibreglass binding around it to stop little bits coming off. I just kept patching it up, and I think it's now in the Melbourne Cricket Ground museum.

Undoubtedly Chappell's most preposterous victory as Australian captain occurred in the 1973 Test against the West Indies at Port-of-Spain, Trinidad. Mostly anchored to the crease by a sprained ankle, hobbling Ian stuck it out for almost four hours to score 97 in the second innings in spite of the world's top off spinner, Lance Gibbs, screwing the ball at deceptive heights off a powdering wicket while two fielders waited in the leg-trap for the seemingly inevitable catch. Chappell recalls:

> Two days before the Test I was playing tennis at the Queen's Park ground when John Benaud wrong-footed me. Over I went. I'd done my ankle — sprained it. I had some treatment, and went to a cocktail party that night

where I had half a dozen beers, maybe more. When Rodney Marsh suggested I wouldn't be able to run on the ankle, I said, 'No, no, look at this,' and I fell flat on my face. The next day at practice I went for a run away from the press and it still wasn't too flash.

In the first innings I put myself at six because I didn't want to go in early and not be able to run too much and just hold things up. Greg went in at three and Dougie Walters at four. That's the day Doug whipped up a century between lunch and tea to score 112, while I tried to play Inshan Ali from the crease and was out caught and bowled.

Stuff this, I thought. I'm not batting at six in the second innings. I'm going in at bloody three. So I had my ankle strapped and out I went and got 97. I took a lot of satisfaction from that as I had to make a few compensations because I wasn't as fleet of foot as usual. Gibbs was turning a lot, and I had to play largely from the crease. I'd go down the track every now and then just to make them think I could do it when I wanted to. However, when I charged, I just blocked the ball rather than hitting a full-blooded shot. Rod Marsh always says the two innings he enjoyed most when he was playing were Dougie's 100 in the first innings and my 90-odd in the second.

By lunch on the last day the West Indians needed 66 runs for victory with five wickets left, including left-hander Alvin Kallicharran on 91. Trinidadians were betting how many wickets would still be standing when the winning run came to square the series at 1-all. In a sweltering dressing room, nobody had any appetite for the braised meat and rice lunches. Over to Chappell:

It's the first and probably the only time when I was captain that I heard our blokes starting to whinge a bit. Whingeing about guys playing and missing or edges that weren't carrying or going wide. When you're the captain and you hear your blokes start to complain like that, you know you're looking down the barrel.

I just lay there with my cap over my face wondering what to say. In my book, if you can't say anything sensible, don't say anything at all. There was no point in thumping the table at a time like this. When the umpires came in, I got up. 'If you feel like complaining, forget it,' I said. 'Things won't get better. Just remember there's no prize for second. This'd be a bloody good one to win.'

With that, the Australian players filed back onto the field and Kallicharran nicked Max Walker's first ball after lunch into Marsh's gloves. Chappell recalls:

It was the wicket we wanted. As so often happens, once you get a breakthrough things seem to fall into place. Tangles Walker, who keeps at it and at it, was the ideal bowler and Kerry O'Keeffe did his part by utilising a hole in the wicket. The boys kept up the pressure in the field and things turned our way. We got their last five wickets for 21.

When I compared this Houdini-like escape to when Pakistan was bowled out for 106 after needing only 159 for victory at the SCG, with Max Walker taking 6 for 15, Chappell shook his head. 'No, I always felt we had a chance in that one. One of the Melbourne papers called them Panic-stan and that was spot on.'

Although he disagreed sharply with Sir Donald Bradman over a few things, Chappell claims his relationship with the great man was never that of schoolmaster and pupil. He says:

In fact, Don once gave me some terrific advice. He just said, 'You used to have a good hook shot. What's happened to it?' Bobby Simpson in South Africa in 1966–67 told me to stop hooking, so I was getting into no man's land. I'd instinctively get into position to hook and then have to play the ball chest-on, which caused all sorts of problems. So on the advice of Sir Donald Bradman, I started hooking again.

In a coup d'etat worthy of the colonels of Africa or Latin America, Bill Lawry was dumped as Australia's skipper and opening bat for the seventh Test against Ray Illingworth's Englishmen in Sydney in 1971 and the captaincy given to Chappell. Lawry learnt of his axing on the radio, and Ian was staggered by the lack of sensitivity shown by ACB officials. He says:

When I first got the news, I didn't believe it. I got home that night and said to my first wife Kay, 'The bastards will never get me like they got Bill.'

Although I was vice-captain at the time, I figured I wasn't a unanimous choice because I'd been told in South Africa in 1969 that I'd never captain Australia. The bloke who told me had been told by a Board member. Obviously that Board member didn't have as much pull as he thought because 12 months later I got the job.

Still, I wouldn't win a popularity poll of Board members. I knew I had to get some good results fairly quickly.

I'm lucky because I tend to see the positive side of things. I can look at a glass and see it half full instead of half empty. Hang on, I thought. I'm taking over an Australian side that hasn't won for nine Tests. If I happen to win a game or two straight off, they'll say, Christ, this bloke's a genius. I had everything to win and nothing to lose.

The captains I'd played under had been Les Favell for South Australia and Bobby Simpson and Bill Lawry for Australia. What did I like about their captaincy and what didn't I like? I'd try to do the good things and I figured that if I didn't fancy something, most other people wouldn't like it either. So those were the things I'd avoid. The rest was just commonsense and putting your own personality on the job.

I think there are three parts to captaincy. One, you've got to maintain a decent standard of playing. Kim Hughes made the mistake of trying to divorce his batting from the captaincy. You can't do this because it comes with the territory.

Secondly, you have to place the field and change the bowlers, which is basically commonsense stuff. You don't have to be any Einstein. Greg and I were lucky to have the best cricket education you could possibly have, and we were lucky in the genes, too. There obviously was something there from Vic.

To me, the third part of captaincy is the job you do off the field. Spending time with the players, helping them with any cricketing or personal worry they might have. I liked a beer and a chat in the dressing room or back at the pub, so this was no big deal.

As a captain, you're only as good as the other ten players. You've got to have them pulling behind you.

I fought the fight for the players off the field and I've got no regrets. I think it helped gain the loyalty and respect of the guys and the effort I got on the field. Now I won't say I get invitations to all their weddings and birthday parties. I'm not the best of friends with everyone I captained, but we respected each other and if I asked for something, it would be done.

I short-circuited a few problems by telling guys what I expected of them. Take Doug Walters. When I took over the captaincy, I said, 'Mate, I just want you to play your natural game as soon as you come in. I don't give a stuff if we're 4 for 400 or 4 for 40. If you get out first ball flashing outside the off stump, you'll get no kick in the arse from me.'

I didn't want Doug going out there at 4 for 40, getting halfway through trying to cut the first ball and thinking, 'I shouldn't be doing this.' As soon as you're in two minds, you're gone.

If Doug thought the first ball was meant to be cut, I wanted him to cut it. He might just belt us out of trouble, which he did a couple of times and won us Test matches. If we're 4 for 40 and Doug goes nick and we're 5 for 40, well, it's not Dougie's fault. It's the fault of the blokes who went before him.

I was never a captain who walked around asking people what they thought we should be doing. As soon as you do that, they think, 'You're the captain. If you don't know what we're supposed to be doing, we're in big trouble.' I never even went to my vice-captain Keith Stackpole and asked, 'What do you think, mate?'

What I did was try to create an atmosphere where guys felt comfortable coming up with an idea. You might say, 'Well, here's what I'm doing at the moment — I'll keep going with it for another three or four overs. If nothing happens, we'll give your plan a shot.' That way, the guy doesn't feel like he's been wiped.

For instance, when Jeff Hammond was playing in his first Test against the West Indies at Sabina Park in 1973, he came up and said, 'I want to bounce Kallicharran.'

'Shit, mate,' I said, 'He's a good hooker and this is a pretty good track.'

'I think I can bounce him out.'

'Righto, Bomber,' I said, ' At least you've told me. You've got two shots at it. I'll place the field to give you a bit of protection, and if it doesn't work we'll go back to my plan.'

First bouncer, a little glove from Kallicharran, Rodney Marsh caught it and he's out. You never know where your next idea is coming from, maybe even from a kid playing in his first Test match.

Stacky fielded next to me in the slips, and when Illingworth came in at a really vital time on the first day of The Oval Test in 1971, he turned and said, 'Mate, I think it's worth having a third slip for this bloke straight off.'

'Good idea, Stacky.'

We only had two slips at this stage, so I brought Greg in — nick: Illingworth, c G. Chappell, b Lillee 0.

In the first Test of that series on a greentop at Old Trafford, Rodney Marsh came up trumps in a very abrupt way. Up 'til then most of my captaincy had been at the Adelaide Oval where things were pretty basic — give the quickies a few overs with the new ball and bring on the spinners Mallett and Jenner.

With Bob Massie injured, we had Lillee and Colley with the new ball. So I went Lillee, Colley, bit of medium pace from Greg and Beetle Watson, but not too much, and then I had Inverarity and Gleeson bowling their spin stuff.

After the spinners had had a couple of overs in tandem, Rodney Marsh, who wasn't even a third selector on that tour, walked past and said 'Mate, do you mind if I say something?'

'No.'

'You're a bloody idiot. This is the greatest seamer's paradise of all time and you've got two spinners bowling. For Christ's sake, get Greg and Beetle on. Anybody who bowls seam up.'

Well, Rodney was used to keeping in Perth on a wicket where you use plenty of fast bowling. He's right. Every pitch isn't the Adelaide Oval. Sometimes you have to give the medium pacers a good go between the quickies and the spinners.

At least I'd created an atmosphere where guys felt comfortable making a suggestion. Even to the point when one calls the captain a bloody idiot.

At The Oval in 1975, Chappell announced his retirement from the captaincy of Australia after holding the post for a then record 30 Tests. He marked the match, which was drawn, with a personal innings of 192. He recalls:

I got out because I was stuffed. I'd had a complete gutful and wasn't in the right frame of mind to captain a side. In fact, in that Oval Test I'd made up my mind to retire.

If I'd had a six-month break to come back to in the winter and not play any cricket, I might have gone on and captained the side against the touring West Indians. But I played that series under my brother Greg purely because I didn't want to be seen to be getting out because the Windies had some quickies. We won the series 5–1 and I enjoyed it.

Chappell was a prime mover in Kerry Packer's breakaway World Series Cricket, in which he came out of semi-retirement to lead Australia's team. He thus helped ensure that today's Australian cricketer receives a worthwhile financial return for his endeavours.

These days Chappell is a sports commentator, specialising in cricket and golf, at which his handicap has been as low as seven. His philosophy on camera? 'It's not break and enter. I'm knocking on someone's door and asking if I can come in.' Chappell also makes some pertinent and acerbic observations in his weekly newspaper columns.

Walk into his office or his home and you'd never know that he'd played a game of cricket. There is no memorabilia, pictures, anything. As Ian comments:

I haven't got an Australian jumper, an Australian blazer or an Australian cap. My old man grabbed most of it because he knew I'd throw it out. When he died, I think Mum gave most of it to the South Australian Cricket Association.

I know where one cap went, though. I'd got a duck at the Wanderers ground in Jo'burg and just to rub salt into the wounds, as I was walking off this prick grabbed the cap off my head and took off. From that time onwards I took off my cap as soon as I got out, and I'd have my gloves and cap in front of my mouth as I walked out so the TV cameras wouldn't catch me cursing myself for a stupid shot or whatever.

AUSTRALIA v ENGLAND
The Oval, 10–16 August 1972

England

B. Wood c Marsh b Watson	26	lbw b Massie	90
J.H. Edrich lbw b Lillee	8	b Lillee	18
P.H. Parfitt b Lillee	51	b Lillee	18
J.H. Hampshire c Inverarity b Mallett	42	c I. Chappell b Watson	20
B.L. D'Oliveira c G. Chappell b Mallett	4	c I. Chappell b Massie	43
A.W. Greig c Stackpole b Mallett	16	c Marsh b Lillee	29
R. Illingworth c G. Chappell b Lillee	0	lbw b Lillee	31
A.P.E. Knott c Marsh b Lillee	92	b Lillee	63
J.A. Snow c Marsh b Lillee	3	c Stackpole b Mallett	14
G.G. Arnold b Inverarity	22	lbw b Mallett	4
D.L. Underwood not out	3	not out	0
Sundries	17		26
	284		356

	O	M	R	W	O	M	R	W
Lillee	24.2	7	58	5	32.2	8	123	5
Massie	27	5	69	0	32	10	77	2
Watson	12	4	23	1	19	8	32	1
Mallett	23	4	80	3	23	7	66	2
G. Chappell	2	0	18	0				
Inverarity	4	0	19	1	15	4	32	0

Fall of wickets
First innings: 25, 50, 133, 142, 145, 145, 159, 181 262, 284
Second innings: 56, 81, 114, 194, 205, 270, 271, 333, 356, 356

Australia

G.D. Watson c Knott b Arnold	13	lbw b Arnold	6
K.R. Stackpole b Snow	18	c Knott b Greig	79
I.M. Chappell b Snow b Arnold	118	c sub (R. Willis) b Underwood	37
G.S. Chappell c Greig b Illingworth	113	lbw b Underwood	16
R. Edwards b Underwood	79	lbw b Greig	1
A.P. Sheahan c Hampshire b Underwood	5	not out	44
R.W. Marsh b Underwood	0	not out	43
R.J. Inverarity c Greig b Underwood	28		
A.A. Mallett run out	5		
R.A.I. Massie b Arnold	4		
D.K. Lillee not out	0		
Sundries	16		
	399		5 for 242

	O	M	R	W	O	M	R	W
Arnold	35	11	87	3	15	5	26	1
Snow	34.5	5	111	1	6	1	21	0
Greig	18	9	25	0	25.3	10	49	2
D'Oliveira	9	4	17	0				
Underwood	38	16	90	4	35	11	94	2
Illingworth	17	4	53	1	8.5	2	26	0
Parfitt					2	0	10	0

Fall of wickets
First innings: 24, 34, 235, 296, 310, 310, 383, 387, 399, 399
Second innings: 16, 132, 136, 137, 171

Australia won by five wickets

GREG CHAPPELL

Far and away Australia's most cultured stroke-player of modern times,
Greg Chappell whips one away to leg.

GREG CHAPPELL

'All ease and elegance, fit to play before the Queen in Her Majesty's parlour.' John Arlott

Sleeves down and playing with straight-backed, elegant, haughty detachment, Greg Chappell offered a resounding finale to the Test arena which might well have been scripted by a drama producer.

When he hit up 182 in his last Test innings against Pakistan at Sydney Cricket Ground in January 1984, Chappell eclipsed Sir Donald Bradman as Australia's highest Test run-getter, with 7110 at an average of 53.86 to Sir Donald's 6996, and became the only player to score a century both on his Test debut and in his last innings. (Allan Border has since broken Chappell's record for the highest Test runs for Australia.)

On top of that Greg snapped up three catches to break Colin Cowdrey's world record by two with 122 Test catches, as well as taking 47 Test wickets with medium-paced swingers and cutters. With poise and style, Chappell numbered four double centuries among his 24 Test 100s, while four times he got a century in each innings on the way to 74 centuries in first class games, which don't include his 1426 runs in World Series Cricket Super-Tests.

For a non-seeker of records, tall (6 ft 2 in/188 cm), slender Chappell made a habit of turning history on its head. Other world marks he held when he quit the game were:

- World record for most runs in a Test match — 380 (247 not out and 133) against New Zealand at Wellington in 1973–74, which was eclipsed by England's Graham Gooch with 456 (333 and 123) against India at Lord's in 1990.
- World record seven catches in a Test when the ball followed him around everywhere against England in Perth in 1974; subsequently equalled by India's Yajuvendra Singh, whose seven catches, by all reports, may not all have touched the bat.
- In his first Test as captain, he scored a century in each innings (123 and 109 not out) against Clive Lloyd's West Indians in Brisbane in 1975 to set another world mark.
- Captained Australia a record 48 times in his 88 Tests.

But such statistics tell only half the Greg Chappell story. He was far and away the most cultured stroke-player of modern times and, according to many, the finest stylist Australia has produced since the immortal Victor Trumper.

When Chappell clipped the ball off his toes wide of mid-wicket, he did it with a poise and grace and grandeur that has seldom been matched in the long litany of cricket's lore.

Writing a profile on Greg in most perceptive terms in the *Sydney Morning Herald*, actress Kate Fitzpatrick said:

> He's pretty impressive. Tall, lean, erect, proud, dark, strong and silent. He looks broody and mysterious. He has an absolutely wonderful back, completely straight without being rigid.
>
> Greg has thick, dark, very curly hair and big, deep-blue eyes that miss nothing. He is warm, friendly, charming, well-mannered, humorous, sensitive, devoted to his wife and family, earthy and honest. He's a very Aussie hero, a bargain whatever way you look. Mrs Chappell is a very lucky woman.

Ian Chappell's younger brother was born on 7 August 1948, a week before Sir Donald Bradman made a duck in his final Test innings against England at The Oval. According to his mother, Greg could keep a straight bat before he could read.

Ian was touring South Africa when the Adelaide Oval scoreboard used his nameplate for Greg's first match for South Australia at the age of 18. Batting sixth, the youth scored 53 and 62 not out in a manner which suggested he was something special.

Advice from Sir Donald Bradman influenced Chappell to bring the back of his top hand around from the front of the handle, to give a fuller swing-through of the blade for off-side shots. It certainly didn't weaken the on-side strokes which so delighted aficionados. Greg recalls:

> In those days I was strong on the leg side — not the off. Sir Donald was a South Australian selector, but he didn't speak to anyone really except Ashley Mallett, the best spinner I've seen. Anyway he walked through as usual and I said, 'Good morning, Sir Donald.'
>
> He stopped, turned and said, 'You'll never be a good player with a grip like that.' I asked if he had any suggestions. He did and showed me and said it'd feel uncomfortable at first, but it would be easier with practice. He walked off, but stopped at the door and said, 'I've only given this bit of advice to one other player. He didn't take it, and he's no longer in the team.' I rushed to the nets. It was uncomfortable but it got easier. It's the grip I used ever since.

Many years later, when asked to choose a team of the best Australian players since World War II, Sir Donald picked both Greg and Ian Chappell along with himself, Bob Simpson, Arthur Morris, Neil Harvey, Keith Miller, Richie Benaud, Alan Davidson, Ray Lindwall and Don Tallon.

Five months after turning 21 and steeled by a couple of seasons in English county cricket with Somerset, Chappell made 129 and 156 not out against Queensland in Brisbane to become the youngest post-war player to post a century in each innings in Australia.

He figured in an odd incident that season in Adelaide when he bowled a ball which hit a sparrow in flight, killing it instantly. The ball went on to hit John Inverarity's stumps. Believing he was out, the Western Australian headed for the pavilion, but umpire Col Egar ruled the ball was dead and recalled him to the crease.

After Chappell carved 102 off 100 balls against Ray Illingworth's touring English team in 1970, a Test call was simply a matter of time. Given a place in Perth for the second Test at 22, he hit a wonderful century in his first Test innings after John Snow and Peter Lever had got five Australians out for 107 in reply to England's 397.

Beginning patiently and sensibly, Greg joined Ian Redpath in a double-century stand to pull Australia out of deep water. As the evening shadows lengthened, Chappell's second 50 took an hour, with several of the fours in his 108 (there were ten in all) sailing over close-in fielders on the leg side. The century prompted Chappell to note: 'Maybe I'll be Greg Chappell from now on, not Ian's younger brother or Victor Richardson's grandson.'

After losing the first Test of the 1972 English tour when twice bowled out for less than moderate scores, Australia was in awful trouble at Lord's when England, out for 272, grabbed the first two wickets for only seven runs. Into the crisis strode Chappell, slim, erect and purposeful, to play what he regards as the innings of his life.

Joining brother Ian at the crease, he helped rally the innings until Ian departed with the score of 82; Doug Walters was out almost at once for one. The score was then 4 for 84. Chappell batted with technical mastery and courage, with the emphasis almost solely on survival. No boundary came for almost three hours, his longest wait for a four.

With Ross Edwards replacing Walters, Chappell chose to attack. It was as if he had decided that the initiative had to be wrested from the Englishmen and he dismissed John Snow, John Price, Tony Greig, Norman Gifford and Ray Illingworth to all parts of the ground. Several times Chappell thrust his left foot down the pitch and smashed fast man Price up the ground for four. With Edwards playing a limpet-like supporting role, Greg scored all but ten of their 50 partnership with upright and regal stroke-play. Edwards was finally out with the total of 190, having made only 28 of the 106 runs he and Chappell had put on for the fifth wicket.

With staunch support from old crony Rod Marsh, Chappell finally went for 131 to a standing ovation when the score was 250, but by then Australia was on the way to a first innings lead of 36. Bob Massie destroyed England's second innings for 116 by taking 8 for 53 and Australia was left with a mere 81 to square the series.

Ever conscious of his side's dependence on his wicket staying intact, Chappell batted through six chanceless hours punctuated with 14 fours in an innings which coupled brave defence and imperious stroke-play. Jack Fingleton was moved to write: 'His strokes were glorious . . . I have seen many great innings by Australians, but none I have admired more than this one by Greg Chappell. Long may he prosper.'

In the final Test at The Oval, Chappell entered with Australia 2 for 34, but this time he needed only three hours for his century, hitting 14 fours in his 113 as he figured in a partnership of 201 with brother Ian, who got 118.

Explaining why his 131 at Lord's was so special, Chappell says:

> Well, it was my first Test at Lord's for one thing. As a kid, I listened to all the Tests on radio and fell in love with Lord's and the Sydney Cricket Ground, so by the time I got to Lord's I knew exactly what it would be like. The headquarters of cricket. The Long Room. The atmosphere at Lord's is unbelievable, particularly on Test match morning, but you can play there when it's empty and still get a buzz. It's the same with the SCG.
>
> We'd been utterly outplayed in the first Test on a seaming wicket, and we struck similar conditions on the first two days at Lord's. The atmosphere was heavy and overcast, helping the ball to swing and seam. It was very difficult for batting.
>
> From the start of the innings I found myself in a state of mind that was almost trance-like. I seemed to see everything in slow motion. Every aspect of my batting was tested and I came through with flying colours. Basically what I had to do was stay in as long as I could in a sheet anchor role. Pick off the odd loose ball and wear them down.
>
> Brother Ian got 50-odd and under the conditions it was a quick 50. He went for his shots and did quite a bit of hooking, one of the hook shots going for six before he was out, caught at backward square.
>
> I still can remember two or three of my strokes. A cover drive off Basil d'Oliveira, a square cut for four and a drive down the slope off John Price.

Only once did I play a false shot and that was the one I got out to. I tried to hit d'Oliveira off the back foot and inside-edged it on to my stumps.

I've played a couple of better innings from a stroke-making point of view, but they were in very good batting conditions. My 247 not out against New Zealand in Wellington in 1974, 200 against India in Sydney in the early 80s and 201 against Pakistan in Brisbane. From a stroke-play point of view, they were better.

Another time I got 170-odd in Christchurch, getting 100 in a session when play resumed after the first day. In World Series Cricket I had a couple of good ones, too. At the SCG I got 190-odd and when we toured the West Indies in 1979 I got three 100s and a 90 in four innings. I never played better than I did that month, but as the games weren't official they tend to slip from memory. The bowling was as good as any I've faced, but it's funny how your subconscious tends to forget some of those World Series 100s because of that word 'official'.

My Test debut 108 in Perth is right up there, too, but mainly because of the occasion. It was a much better batting wicket than the one at Lord's. With John Snow bowling well, it wasn't easy in the early stages, but the conditions got better and better. Ian Redpath was up the other end doing the donkey work. Redders shielded me from the better bowling early in the day, but at Lord's it was up to me to take the best bowling.

Interestingly enough, I rate a 50-odd [Greg scored 40 out of 138] I got in the first innings of the 1977 Centenary Test in Melbourne as one of my best innings. Under difficult conditions in a low-scoring game I felt it was an innings to be proud of.

As time went on, Chappell became increasingly strong on the off side, and by the end of his career he seemed to score the majority of his runs there. Because of the prevalence of short-pitched fast bowling in the 1970s, he mastered the cut shot. Chances to use his matchless on-drive almost dried up because bowlers were, not surprisingly, reluctant to pitch the ball up on his legs.

After becoming the first Australian to top 1000 runs on a tour of the West Indies in 1973, Chappell figured in a fraternal run-spree with brother Ian in the Wellington Test against New Zealand in 1974, becoming the first brothers to score a century in each innings of a Test. Greg notched up 247 not out and 133 while Ian scored 145 and 121.

After watching South Africa's Graeme Pollock demolish Australia's bowlers with a heavy bat when he toured here with a World XI in 1971–72, Chappell himself decided to switch to a heavier model. He explains:

> I'd always used a lightish bat, but when I saw how effortlessly Pollock hit the ball to the boundary with his heavy bat, I got Gray Nicolls to jump me up to 2lb 8oz and then 2lb 12oz. Seeing I was basically a straight player, not a hooker or cutter, I thought it would work for me, too. But by the end of my career I was back to 2lb 6oz.
>
> I used to get two new bats a year, but never let myself have a favourite in case I lost it or broke it. I've seen guys go to pieces because they lost a favourite bat. Funnily, I never broke a bat in my life. The only casualty was one that split through dry rot after I'd left it in my bag through the winter months.

After transferring to Queensland for the 1973–74 season, Greg (at 27) took over the Australian captaincy from Ian and promptly beat Clive Lloyd's outstandingly strong West Indies team 5–1 in 1975–76. In the stuff schoolboys' dreams are made of, Chappell became the first incoming Test captain to score a century in each innings in a first-up victory in Brisbane. With Ian generously giving him the strike with frequently taken singles, Greg scored a chanceless 109 not out off 172 balls on a sharply turning wicket in the second innings. After losing his first Test toss, Greg promptly won five successive Test tosses from Lloyd using a 1902 penny, a two-up relic. He finished the series with 702 runs at the Bradman-like average of 117.

In spite of having an extremely strong-willed elder brother playing under him, Greg refused to become an imitation of Ian. He was less extrovert, having a mind of his own as he handled the team coolly and firmly.

If there is one thing Chappell regrets about his marvellous career, it is that infamous day in Melbourne in 1981 when New Zealand needed a six off the last ball to win a crucial one-dayer. Greg ordered brother Trevor to bowl an underarm daisy-cutter along the ground. Chappell claims his action was caused by frustration and annoyance with the administrators rather than meanness of spirit.

> There was no consideration for the players. We had no right to an opinion. Look, six off the last ball was a million to one chance. Winning for us meant a couple of days off, a luxury, that's all. I was wrong. I regret it. I wouldn't do it again. I was shattered at the outrage and screaming chaos that followed. I'm stuck with it . . . but it wasn't illegal.

In spite of his great natural ability, sound technique and superb temperament, Chappell went through a horror stretch in 1981–82 in which he made seven ducks in fairly rapid succession. Greg himself feels the problem was essentially a mental one, and indeed he scored another five Test centuries before his retirement.

Old friend Rod Marsh comments:

> That summer of failures was the making of Greg Chappell. He had always been a perfectionist who would not tolerate fools. It would upset him if one of his team made a fielding error or bowled a bad ball. Everyone makes mistakes, but Greg always has been one of the great players and he found it difficult to understand why all those around him were not similarly blessed. Those ducks taught Greg that he is, after all, only human and that those around him are mere mortals too.

In view of Chappell's superlative 182 in his final Test innings, does he ever feel he pulled the pin too early?

> Let's face it, I overdosed on cricket. I got to the stage where I wasn't enjoying it, so I knew my time was up. I struggled through my last season in 1984 and couldn't get pumped up. In the Adelaide Test against Pakistan, my mind went blank and I ran myself out. I hit a ball to cover, called and was out by three or four yards. I just wasn't thinking. As I walked off in a daze, I knew the time had come to give the game away.
>
> When Ian retired just before World Series Cricket, I said, 'How can you give it away? Cricket has been your life for so long.' Ian replied, 'Mate, no one will have to tell you. You know when your time is up.' Well, my time had arrived.
>
> In the Melbourne Test I struggled because my heart wasn't in it. I realised the only way to get myself motivated for the Sydney Test was to announce my retirement before it started. Now I'd closed all gates, I could build myself up for one last hurrah.
>
> Actually I'd struggled mentally for a season and a half. One of the strongest points of my game was my capacity to concentrate, and it was getting harder and harder at the mental level.
>
> I reckoned there were three levels of concentration, starting with alert. Waiting to go out to bat, between balls, being aware of what's going on around you. When the bowler turned to begin his run-up, you tune in to a finer level of concentration like you were watching things on a TV screen. As the bowler ran up, I'd take a good look at his face. You can learn a lot from that.
>
> When the bowler got to his delivery stride, my concentration reached the level of fierce. I'm watching the ball in the air so fiercely for a fraction of a second that I felt I was burning holes in it. I could see right through it. That's how it should be when you're highly motivated. Nothing can disturb you. After each ball, I'd drop two levels back to alert.

> A lot has been made of sledging, the mental warfare bit. It happened a bit in my early days, but the guys gave up on me when they realised I didn't get upset. You try them out, though. Sometimes sledging is the worst thing you can do, particularly to a guy like Viv Richards. With Viv, you'd try not to upset him. He might be struggling to get his head together, and if you gave him the needle, he'd grit his teeth and say, 'Bugger you, I'll show you.'
>
> I had no trouble slipping in and out of the various levels of concentration. I've seen guys walk off the field drained at the end of the day, but I could keep concentrating for ages without any ill effects. Even after a helter-skelter World Series game, I'd have a few beers, walk into the hotel, have a shower and be asleep as soon as my head hit the pillow. Maybe it's because I've got no brains.

Of course, nobody would ever accuse Gregory Stephen Chappell of having no brains as he has become a millionaire through shrewd business foresight and the knack of picking the right partners. Apart from insurance and real estate, he has been involved in hotels, a travel agency, mango plantations, a goldmine and jojoba — a Mexican plant that promises to be a viable substitute for sperm whale oil as an additive to cosmetics and motor oil. He has also had stints as an Australian selector and as a radio and television commentator.

Having cut his ties with cricket administration, Chappell turned to golf at which he has a seven handicap at Royal Queensland. He says, 'I'm past the fanatic stage, and now I'm a keen student of the game. I can't learn enough about it. I love talking about golf, reading about it and watching good players.' One day Greg hopes to qualify for the Australian amateur championship.

Although he faced up to the fierce deliveries of Dennis Lillee, John Snow, Joel Garner, Andy Roberts and Michael Holding, Chappell rates England spinner Derek Underwood as the most difficult bowler he has faced. He explains:

> Underwood has got me out more times than any other bowler in Test cricket, but I suppose he's bowled more balls at me than anyone else. Given the right conditions, I'd back him to bowl out any Test team in the world. Dennis Lillee was a great bowler under any conditions. I batted against him in a lot of Sheffield Shield matches, and he was always coming up with different ways to get you out.

Apart from his magnificent 131 in 1972, Chappell will never forget another magical moment while he was batting in another match at Lord's. When drinks were brought on, the twelfth man handed him a wire service picture of wife Judy and his newly born son Stephen. Learning of the birth that way had him near tears in the centre of the cradle of cricket.

AUSTRALIA v ENGLAND
Lord's, 22–26 June 1972

England

G. Boycott b Massie	11	b Lillee	6
J.H. Edrich lbw b Lillee	10	c Marsh b Massie	6
B.W. Luckhurst b Lillee	1	c Marsh b Lillee	4
M.J.K. Smith b Massie	34	c Edwards b Massie	30
B.L. d'Oliveira lbw b Massie	32	c G. Chappell b Massie	3
A.W. Greig c Marsh b Massie	54	c I. Chappell b Massie	3
A.P.E. Knott c Colley b Massie	43	c G. Chappell b Massie	12
R. Illingworth lbw b Massie	30	c Stackpole b Massie	12
J.A. Snow b Massie	37	c Marsh b Massie	0
N. Gifford c Marsh b Massie	3	not out	16
J.S.E. Price not out	4	c G. Chappell b Marsh	19
Sundries	13		5
	272		116

	O	M	R	W	O	M	R	W
Lillee	28	3	90	2	21	6	50	2
Massie	32.5	7	84	8	27.2	9	53	8
Colley	16	2	42	0	7	1	8	0
G. Chappell	6	1	18	0				

Fall of wickets
First innings: 22, 23, 28, 84, 97, 193, 200, 260, 265, 272
Second innings: 12, 16, 18, 25, 31, 52, 74, 74, 81, 116

Australia

K.R. Stackpole c Gifford b Price	5	not out	57
B.C. Francis b Snow	0	c Knott b Price	9
I.M. Chappell c Smith b Snow	56	c Luckhurst b d'Oliveira	6
G.S. Chappell b d'Oliveira	131	not out	7
K.D. Walters c Illingworth b Snow	1		
R. Edwards c Smith b Illingworth	28		
J.W. Gleeson c Knott b Greig	1		
R.W. Marsh c Greig b Snow	50		
D.J. Colley c Greig b Price	25		
R.A.L. Massie c Knott b Snow	0		
D.K. Lillee not out	2		
Sundries	9		2
	308		2 for 81

	O	M	R	W	O	M	R	W
Snow	32	13	57	5	8	2	15	0
Price	26.1	5	87	2	7	0	28	1
Greig	29	6	74	1	3	0	17	0
d'Oliveira	17	5	48	1	8	3	14	1
Gifford	11	4	20	0				
Illingworth	7	2	13	1				
Luckhurst					0.5	0	5	0

Fall of wickets
First innings: 1, 7, 82, 84, 190, 212, 250, 290, 290, 308
Second innings: 20, 51

Australia won by 8 wickets

RODNEY MARSH

Even if he didn't keep wicket, many consider that Rodney Marsh had the skills to play for Australia purely as a batsman.

RODNEY MARSH

'Rodney Marsh might hit sixes, but he is not a slogger. I would call him a Very Scientific Hard Hitter.'
Jack Fingleton

With a picture of Australia's first wicketkeeper, Jack Blackham, in his hip pocket, Rodney Marsh hit a century for the history books with an unbeaten 110 in the Centenary Test against England in Melbourne in 1977. It was the first 100 hit by an Australian wicketkeeper off England and came as a follow-up to West Australia's Marsh breaking Wally Grout's Australian record of 187 victims when he caught John Lever off Dennis Lillee in England's first innings.

Squat as a rugby scrum-half, with bulging thighs, a blacksmith's forearms and a gymnast's spring heels, Marsh finished his 96-Test career with a world record 355 scalps. This figure doesn't include the 48 catches he took in 15 World Series Cricket Super-Tests in 1977–79, games of vastly superior quality to the Test matches of the time.

Although Olympic swimmer Neil Brooks is said to have subsequently broken his mark, Marsh set another record by quaffing 45 tinnies of beer on the flight to England for the 1983 World Cup.

Inked into the Test scorebook no less than 95 times was the legend c Marsh b Lillee, a stunning figure when you realise Australia's number two duo was Wally Grout and Alan Davidson with 54. Fittingly, it was Lillee who provided the brute of a ball from which Marsh caught archrival Ian Botham at Leeds in 1981 to break Alan Knott's world record 263 victims. ' I'd be less than honest if I denied feeling as tall as Joel Garner,' he admits.

Not long after Marsh had returned to the dressing room, a bottle of champagne arrived with a note: 'Congratulations. Well deserved. I hope you don't drop this one.' It was from a sporting Alan Knott.

The first congratulatory call came from Ian Chappell, who bubbled down the line: 'Congratulations, pal. I'll just repeat what Dougie Walters said when you broke Wally Grout's record in the Centenary Test. If you'd held on to all those catches in your first Test match, you'd have passed Knottie's record months ago.'

Chappell and Walters were harking back to Marsh's horror debut against England in Brisbane in 1970 when he dropped three catches, none of them sitters. Word came through that the English XI had nicknamed him Iron Gloves; Marsh's self-criticism was almost as harsh. Feeling unworthy of the Australian cap, he left it in his locker and finished the Brisbane Test bareheaded.

The howls from the critics and jeers of the crowds in Brisbane and Sydney were deplorable; it was hardly Marsh's fault that he leapfrogged over NSW's Brian Taber and Queensland's John McLean on the strength of his superior batting after only 13 first class matches. However, a big heart and an unquenchable sense of humour brought Marsh through without his nerve cracking.

He recalls:

> The press and the Poms gave it to me in large lumps when I dropped three or four catches, none of which were simple but all of which should have been caught. I felt worse for being shown up by Alan Knott keeping like a dream. That Iron Gloves tag took a bit of getting over.
>
> I think it was Sir Donald Bradman who got me selected. He came to watch a Shield game in Brisbane a couple of weeks before the Test team was chosen, and I thought it strange a big man like him would go all that way. I got half a dozen catches and 50 something, and I think it was my batting that got me the spot. In South Africa the year before it had been sort of five out, all out.
>
> Apart from Garth McKenzie, I hardly knew a soul when I went to Brisbane for that Test. After practice I went out to play golf with Ian Chappell, Doug Walters and Ray Lindwall. I've never forgotten that, because Ray's was the only autograph I've ever got in my life. He was my idol when I was a 10- or 11-year-old kid, and I remember running across the WACA to get him to sign. Ten years down the track, here I was playing golf and having a beer with the great man.

Born on 4 November 1947, Rodney William Marsh (nicknamed Bacchus after the Western Australian team's train stopped at a Victorian country station called Bacchus Marsh) is five years younger than brother Graham, whose golfing deeds in Japan have made him a millionaire a few times over.

So that he could keep wickets for the WA University club, Rod entered an Arts course. While a third-year student, he scored 104 for Western Australia against the West Indies at the age of 20, standing on the left-hand side of the bat. He is a right-hander in everything else, including golf and tennis.

Marsh now lives in Adelaide, where he is head of the Australian Institute of Sport's Cricket Academy, and was preparing for the April 1991 intake of the country's most gifted young cricketers when I raised the subject of his most gratifying century. Typically, he said:

> Truly, personal records have never been my big go. I just remember the Test matches that we won. Any innings I played or catch I took that didn't go towards winning or saving a Test don't matter. The three times I hit a Test century [132 against New Zealand, 118 against Pakistan and 110 not out against England], we won the match and that's what meant the most to me. It's not what you do individually. I know my century against Pakistan in Adelaide in '72–73 was the first by an Australian wicketkeeper in a Test, but the only thing I remember about it was that we won the game.

But when Marsh's grandchildren call upon him to tell them about some of his moments of cricketing glory, he surely will begin with the Centenary Test in 1977 when, as Australia's vice-captain, he scored 138 runs and snared five catches, including the one that took him past Wally Grout's Australian record. Marsh recalls:

> Just before the game I got a letter from one of the granddaughters of Jack Blackham, who was Australia's wicketkeeper in that very first Test match back in 1877. Enclosed with it was a tiny picture of him. I put it in my back pocket and forgot about it until I'd been out on the field for a while. I kept it there for the rest of the match.
>
> For some reason I struck really good form with the bat in that Test, and not just when I got 110 not out in the second innings. Greg Chappell batted four hours for 40-odd in the first innings, so it wasn't easy, I can tell you. I got 28, the next best score, and hit the ball really well.
>
> In the second innings the pitch was a lot easier to play on and everybody's nerves had settled down. It was a mighty big occasion with almost every living English and Australian Test player flying in for the game and Queen Elizabeth meeting the guys.
>
> I can't recall a lot of shots, but that 110 not out was the best 100 I ever got. I was at the other end when David Hookes hit Tony Greig for five successive fours. A few looks and a few words were exchanged, but bugger all actually.
>
> I do remember trying to sweep spinner Derek Underwood and nearly dragging the ball on to my stumps. Underwood bowled only 12 overs in the second innings, which was ridiculous. He was conscious of his average, but he always threw a few up to me. Underwood didn't like bowling to left-handers, but he knew I fancied my chances of putting him over the fence if I got the opportunity. He always had a chance of getting me if he tossed one up.
>
> I couldn't believe it when Rick McCosker came in with his broken jaw strapped up at the fall of the eighth wicket because I thought we had enough at that stage. He didn't want me to miss a chance of getting a century on such an occasion and Bob Willis was quick to bounce one at him.

> I did pretty well, but that wasn't important. It was such a brilliant game of cricket. It had everything for those of us privileged to play. England had a chance to close the game up and play for a draw after tea on the final day, but they continued to go for the runs and the occasion was all the richer for that decision. In the end we won by 45 runs, exactly the same margin by which Australia had won the first Test 100 years earlier.

Bristling with belligerence, whether batting or taking more punishment than any wicketkeeper can have done as he kept wicket to Dennis Lillee and Jeff Thomson, Marsh had become known as an irreplaceable component in Australia's winning formula. England's Ian Wooldridge declared: 'In the great Australian tradition, Rodney Marsh gives the impression that he'd lay you cold first and then buy you a reviving beer.' Without fail he'd celebrate an Australian Test victory by leaping naked onto a dressing room table and shouting,

> Beneath the Southern Cross I stand
> A sprig of wattle in my hand
> A native of my native land
> Australia, you bloody beauty.

When Marsh was in the mood, he could be a holy terror with the bat. In 1975–76 he needed only 11 strokes (three sixes, eight fours) to reach 50 against the West Indies, while in 1980–81 he carved 26 runs from Lance Cairns' final over in a World Series Cup game against New Zealand in Adelaide.

Marsh's thunderous 236 runs for WA against Pakistan in 1972–73 remains the second highest score by a wicketkeeper in Australian first class cricket. When the outplayed Australians were losing dismally at Old Trafford in 1972, Marsh lifted their spirits with a valiant 91 in which four sixes were smashed into the crowd in a handful of overs.

Marsh has a soft spot for a century he got for Australia's World Series Cricket team against the West Indies in Antigua. He explains: 'It was probably a higher class 100 than the one I got in the Centenary Test and it saved the game for us. They had the customary four fast bowlers — Andy Roberts, Michael Holding, Joel Garner and Colin Croft. We had the helmets by then, thank God.'

In a tribute to his old comrade, Dennis Lillee said:

> I cannot think of anyone who better typified the fighting spirit on a cricket field than Bacchus. I'm certain few people are aware of the pain he suffered

> and the sacrifices he made just to play cricket. In later years, he would limp into the room after each session in a day behind the stumps and pack his arthritic knee in ice. His hands took a terrible pounding, too, never more so than in the 1974–75 season against Mike Denness and his Poms when Jeff Thomson was at his glove-thudding best. Again, no complaints. Nothing — certainly nothing so mundane as injury or pain — was going to interfere with his involvement with Test cricket.

Marsh didn't drop too many catches after his horror Test debut in Brisbane, although he did spill a couple off Terry Alderman in a Prudential Cup game against England at Edgbaston in 1981. When a streaker took to the field, Rod tackled the clown and held him down until the police got there. On the TV highlights that night, Richie Benaud quipped: 'Well, I think that's the first thing Rodney Marsh has caught all day.'

When Greg Chappell stood down from the captain's job after the 1983–84 series against Pakistan, Marsh waited loyally in the wings for a call. A straw poll of Australia's players would have given him the job almost unopposed, but perhaps Rod's outspokenness or links with World Series Cricket told against him, and Kim Hughes took Australia to the West Indies. Marsh promptly pulled the pin on a fabulous career — a pity because his sharp cricketing brain had been honed by playing under such abrasive, inspirational leaders as Tony Lock and Ian Chappell. Marsh says:

> I've got no regrets about retiring when I did. I just woke up one morning and decided I'd had a gutful. I would have gone to the West Indies if I had been captain because that was all that was left for me. Still, I'd had my best ever season with the gloves that summer, so it was a good way to go out. While I was on top.

AUSTRALIA v ENGLAND
Melbourne, 12–17 March 1977

Australia

	First innings		Second innings	
I.C. Davis	lbw b Lever	5	c Knott b Greig	68
R.B. McCosker	b Willis	4	c Greig b Old	25
G.J. Cosier	c Fletcher b Lever	10	c Knott b Lever	4
G.S. Chappell	b Underwood	40	b Old	2
D.W. Hookes	c Greig b Old	17	c Fletcher b Underwood	56
K.D. Walters	c Greig b Willis	4	c Knott b Greig	66
R.W. Marsh	c Knott b Old	28	not out	110
G.J. Gilmour	c Greig b Old	4	b Lever	16
K.J. O'Keeffe	c Brearley b Underwood	0	c Willis b Old	14
D.K. Lillee	not out	10	c Amiss b Old	25
M.H.N. Walker	b Underwood	2	not out	8
Sundries		14		25
		138		9(dec) for 419

	O	M	R	W	O	M	R	W
Lever	12	1	36	2	21	1	95	2
Willis	8	0	33	2	22	0	91	0
Old	12	4	39	3	27.6	2	104	4
Underwood	11.6	2	16	3	12	2	38	1
Greig					14	3	66	2

Fall of wickets
First innings: 11, 13, 23, 45, 51, 102, 114, 117, 136, 138
Second innings: 33, 40, 53, 132, 187, 244, 277, 353, 407

England

	First innings		Second innings	
R.W. Woolmer	c Chappell b Lillee	9	lbw b Walker	12
M.J. Brearley	c Hookes b Lillee	12	lbw b Lillee	43
D.L. Underwood	c Chappell b Walker	7	b Lillee	7
D.W. Randall	c Marsh b Lillee	4	c Cosier b O'Keeffe	174
D.L. Amiss	c O'Keeffe b Walker	4	b Chappell	64
K.W.R. Fletcher	c Marsh b Walker	4	c Marsh b Lillee	1
A.W. Greig	b Walker	18	c Cosier b O'Keeffe	41
A.P.E. Knott	lbw b Lillee	15	lbw b Lillee	42
C.M. Old	c Marsh b Lillee	3	c Chappell b Lillee	2
J.K. Lever	c Marsh b Lillee	11	lbw b O'Keeffe	4
R.G.D. Willis	not out	1	not out	5
Sundries		7		22
		95		417

	O	M	R	W	O	M	R	W
Lillee	13.3	2	26	6	34.4	7	139	5
Walker	15	3	54	4	22	4	83	1
O'Keeffe	1	0	4	0	33	6	108	3
Gilmour	5	0	4	0	4	0	29	0
Chappell					16	7	29	1
Walters					3	2	7	0

Fall of wickets
First innings: 19, 30, 34, 40, 40, 61, 65, 78, 86, 95
Second innings: 28, 113, 279, 290, 346, 369, 380, 385, 410, 417

Australia won by 45 runs

BARRY RICHARDS

South Africa's Barry Richards once scored an unbeaten 325 in a day for South Australia while being paid a dollar per run.

BARRY RICHARDS

'When cricketers scowl and chew gum, the result is highly unattractive. But Barry Richards completes a perfect technical picture of bland assurance unmarred by a rotating jaw.' E.W. Swanton

As Barry Richards sat at his desk at the Queensland Cricket Association, he gazed wistfully up at a picture of the scoreboard at the Western Australian Cricket Association ground in Perth taken in 1970. With the clock showing just after noon on the second day, South Australia's score had become 4 for 551 the instant Richards was out for 356. His innings had been a mixture of arrogance and elegance, emphasising why the South African had been hailed as the world's number one batsman.

Looking down the list of suffering Western Australian bowlers, he said: 'Dennis Lillee, Graham McKenzie, Sticks Brayshaw, Tony Lock, Tony Mann. Not exactly a bunch of mugs. When you're travelling as well as I was that day, you can almost decide where you want to hit the ball.'

Richards came from a generation of South African cricketers who were acceptable alone, but were treated as fiends incarnate if they travelled as a team. He played just four Tests, averaging 72.57 as he thumped the daylights out of Bill Lawry's Australians in 1969–70, when the sports boycott against South Africa took effect and robbed Test cricket of a genius.

As a cosmopolitan mercenary, the 6 ft (183 cm) tall, curly-topped Springbok opening bat continued to pile up the runs for Hampshire, Natal and South Australia, playing countless strokes which left bowlers and spectators alike gasping with astonishment at their beauty, their authority and their elegance of style.

Yet often Richards would become so arrogant in his contempt for the bowling that he would block the half-volleys and dispatch good balls to the boundary. On an easy wicket he would get to 50 and throw away his wicket with a rash stroke, explaining: 'Batting in front of three people on a cold day in Derby while lesser cricketers were playing Tests did bore and annoy me.' Arrogant — yes, but brutally honest. 'You see,' Richards added, 'with due modesty, I've done it all apart from Test cricket, which I can't play now.'

Richards' first-up Test century against Australia in Durban was the most perfect exhibition you could wish to see — the 100 reached four balls after lunch, after a glorious array of quick-footed strokes.

It was proof that when the South African applied himself to the full, his batting was near perfection. Each stroke was played precisely as the textbook directs.

His century in the fourth Test at Port Elizabeth summed up the enigma of a man who sometimes became bored with his own extravagant gifts. Having reached 50-odd with reasonable circumspection and attention to detail, he was pinned down for a few overs and thereafter slogged his way to 126, spectacularly and brilliantly but not always with what the purist would consider a proper adjustment of the feet.

The key to how good he was and how weary of batting he often became lies in his response to how he would have played in his fourth Test had he known it would be his last. 'I would have batted all day,' Richards said. 'They would never have got me out.'

Barry Richards was born on 21 July 1945 in Durban, where within a few months the hospitals and nursing homes also sent forth Graeme Pollock and Mike Proctor. His father ran the municipal market and played rugby.

Richards discovered a talent with the cricket bat at the age of about eight or nine, endlessly hitting a golf ball against the garage wall. That was also how the infant Don Bradman started, although the Don used a stump as a bat.

Richards says: 'I went to Durban High School, but I spent more time in the nets than anywhere. I'm not academic. I don't mind English, but I couldn't take maths or science. I never matriculated because I didn't want to go to university — nor could I have afforded it.'

In England, where in those days they viewed the commercially minded with suspicion, he was sometimes looked upon warily. Making money from cricket was just not cricket. With its strained finances and part amateur traditions, English cricket found it hard to understand a young man unashamedly in the game for money. Richards, equally understandably, argued that if he was one of the best in the world in his field, he deserved to be paid as such.

With opportunities to play Test cricket having gone, Richards came to Australia for the 1970–71 season when the Coca Cola people whetted his appetite by offering him a dollar for every run he scored for South Australia.

That was like handing Dracula the key to the blood bank, and the Springbok promptly set the Australian summer ablaze, with only Sir Donald Bradman topping his 1538 runs at an average of 109.86. To keep him at home with Natal the following year, a Durban ice cream merchant offered four rand a run, and bought $4,000 worth. With the first of his eight centuries for South Australia being a score of 224 against the touring MCC, Richards flew to Perth for the game against Western Australia, which provided the most memorable day's batting.

> On the day before the game I felt quite apprehensive after having a hit in the nets. Every time a bowler slipped himself, the ball flew off the track like lightning. Moreover, the pre-game ballyhoo centred round a young, fiery fast bowler who was on the verge of playing for Australia. Dennis Lillee was his name. He had missed the first match in Adelaide, but now he was to share the new ball with Graham McKenzie — a formidable pairing on a wicket as quick as any in the world.
>
> Ian Chappell won the toss, and I opened with John Causby on a very quick wicket which was hard and shiny. McKenzie's first ball was a gentle outswinger which I played for and missed. As Rod Marsh tossed the ball back, he turned to John Inverarity at first slip and said loudly, 'Geez, I thought this bloke could play a bit.'
>
> That evening when Lillee bowled the last delivery of the day, I walked down the wicket, drove the ball back past him for four and without breaking stride continued towards the pavilion: 325 not out. Invers turned to Marsh and commented cryptically, 'I suppose he can play a bit.'
>
> Rod still jokes that he gave a faultless performance behind the stumps because that first ball from McKenzie was the only one to pass my bat. In fact, as the South Australian players carved up the attack, he brilliantly stumped Ian Chappell for 129 after we had put on 308 in 170 minutes and then threw himself to catch Greg Chappell. Well though Western Australia fielded, we ended up at 3 for 513 after the five and half hours of the opening day. In those days we started at 11.30 rather than the 11 o'clock start they have today.
>
> Recalling that innings now is like a dream. I was never tied down and I kept playing my shots. Somehow I managed to sustain for a complete day the sort of form that usually comes in short, glorious moments. The conditions couldn't have been better, and the quality of the WA attack — which also included Tony Lock, the English spin hero — forced me to keep a higher than usual level of concentration.
>
> The day began with a quarter of an hour of reconnaissance before I got off the mark. A period of adjustment to the pace of the Perth wicket. My first runs came from a square drive off the back foot in the fourth over which I hardly struck, but the ball flew past point for four. So fast did the ball come on to the bat that every nudge sped to the boundary. Those boots with extremely sharp spikes that got John Benaud banned had just come in, yet the wicket was so hard I couldn't get them to grip the turf.

By lunch I had made 79 in a fairly steady manner, but in the next session Ian and I sailed into their spinners. We matched each other shot for shot and I progressed from 100 to 200 in only 84 minutes. With Ian playing so well at the other end, it would have been pointless inviting me to take a single. If they'd put all the fielders back, we would have taken a single off each ball and that's six runs an over. They simply had to keep trying to get us out.

Lockie became more and more frustrated, particularly when he fielded at mid-off to the medium pacers of Sticks Brayshaw. I drove one ball for four which Tony dived at and just missed. So he dropped ten yards deeper for the next. The result was another despairing dive and another four. He backed off still further, but I still managed to place my shot just outside his reach as he flung himself to the ground again.

Still, Brayshaw should have had me out at 169 when I lofted a drive off McKenzie straight to him at mid-on. He missed the catch, but told me later he didn't expect it to be an expensive miss. It looked from my slogging as though I would throw my wicket away at any moment. In fact, it cost Western Australia another 187 runs. The only other chance I gave was from the shot which brought up my triple century. Mind you, only a fielder as athletic as Bob Meuleman, who was a champion squash player, would have got a hand to a miscued, cross-batted shot over cover which finished up at the third man boundary.

As you'd expect, I was on the receiving end of a few curses from Lillee, particularly when I had my moments of fortune against him with a couple of unconvincing hooks which dropped safely and dribbled to the boundary. For the rest, it was a performance that will warm my twilight years. One shot I really treasure occurred when Lillee took the second new ball. When I hit Dennis back over his head, the ball crashed against the top of the sight screen and ricocheted back into the playing area.

One of my real regrets in life is that although two TV stations covered the day's play, neither has any TV recording. The ABC searched high and low in the archives for the two-hour tape, but it had all been wiped off and the tape re-used.

I couldn't believe it. Only the second time a player had scored 300 in a day in Australia and they'd wiped the tape clean. With all the Test cricket being played, somebody at the ABC didn't think it was worth keeping. Possibly they thought the days of Sir Donald Bradman was the golden era to be cherished. It was Bill Ponsford and not Bradman who got the other 300 in a day, back in the 1920s. Ray Robinson, one of the great cricket writers, dug into the history books and found that Ponsford had faced 23 eight-ball overs more than I did.

The only souvenirs I have to show my kids are the picture I have in my office and a Western Australian Cricket Association presentation of a water jug and tray engraved, 'To Barry Richards — 325 in a day. A super knock.'

After being rushed off for several interviews, I spent a surprisingly quiet evening with my team-mates. The elation kept away the tiredness, but painting the town was not really my style, and I had to continue the innings the next day.

I lasted only another 42 minutes, and it took a terrible lbw decision to get me out. Tony Mann had set a far-flung field with the only noticeable gap at fine leg. When he bowled a full toss which was going down the leg side, I tried to paddle the ball into that open space — not an easy shot. I missed and Rocket Mann, a purveyor of almighty appeals in true Australian fashion, gave full vent in his most pleading manner. Warren Carter gave me out, and Rocket and I still maintain he was sick and tired of seeing me at the crease.

Richards finished with 356, having batted for 372 minutes, and for those with a bent for statistics, he scored 100 in 125 minutes, 200 in 209 minutes and 300 in 317 minutes. In all, Richards hit one six and 48 fours. However, the figures that he savoured most belonged to his good friend Dennis Lillee — 18 overs, 1 maiden, 117 runs, no wickets. South Australia then bowled Western Australia out twice for their victory of the season, a result which set Chappell's men on course to become Sheffield Shield champions. Richards added a final postscript to his Perth triumph:

Actually, I nearly figured in a bloodbath the morning after the game. I had persuaded Lorna, my girlfriend of the time who was a former Miss Rhodesia, to fly out to Australia. Because Perth is an international airport and Adelaide is not, we planned her arrival to coincide with the last day of the Western Australia game. Her flight was due around four or five the next morning.

When we won the game, Ian and Greg Chappell and I got stuck into the turps, and when Greg left at two in the morning, I decided it would be pointless going to bed. Ian let me down by nodding off in mid-conversation. Still holding a glass of beer, I popped off as well. Next thing I knew it was six o'clock.

I raced to the airport praying the flight had been delayed, but of course it was right on schedule. Not knowing a soul in the country apart from me, poor Lorna was in a terrible state. It wasn't a happy reunion. In fact, her first words were punctuated with comments which made Dennis Lillee's curses seem rather tame. We finally got to Adelaide to find my flat had been done over by a burglar who obviously read the cricket reports.

Obviously when you are earning a dollar a run, you would not be human if you threw away easy chances of augmenting the income. Richards wound up the Australian season by going in with a broken finger and sharing in a brisk stand which allowed South Australia to declare and win the final match and the Sheffield Shield.

Because of the sheer volume of runs, Richards unhesitatingly rates that 356 as his greatest innings, although from a technical point of view he claims he played just as well in a couple of county matches for Hampshire. He says:

> In only my second game of county cricket, we went to Yorkshire to face Freddie Trueman, Ray Illingworth, Don Wilson and Tony Nicholson, who should have played for England but didn't. Names I held in awe.
>
> Although the wicket at Harrogate was covered where the bowlers delivered the ball, the actual pitch was left bare. This time one of the covers wasn't bolted down properly and it blew down on top of half the wicket. Down came the rain and we had to bat on a dry wicket at one end and a wet one at the other. Quite a scenario. An inexperienced guy coming from South Africa to play in such foreign conditions in freezing weather, I got 70 out of 122.
>
> The second time was against Middlesex when they had to beat us to win the county championship. We told the groundsman to prepare a nice wicket, but he made it too dry and the ball turned square. With England spinners Fred Titmus and Phil Edmonds in the Middlesex attack, I got 59 out of 150, with tail-ender Lofty Herman getting 30-odd just having a slog. Second time round, I batted through the innings for 70 not out out of 130-odd. It was really testing stuff, with Titmus and Edmonds taking 18 of the 20 wickets that fell.

Richards spurned the heavy bats that have become the norm these days, preferring a 2lb $5\frac{1}{2}$ oz model that was a matchstick compared to those used today. He explains this choice:

> In my day a 2lb 4oz bat was quite normal, and it wasn't until Graeme Pollock, Ian Botham and Graham Gooch came along that the heavy bats appeared. I was a touch player rather than a bludgeoner. Playing cuts and glides would have been very difficult with a heavy bat. I'm not a particularly strong person, and I doubt if I could have lifted Clive Lloyd's jumbo bat. Graeme Pollock used heavy bats, but they had the thinnest handle I've ever seen on a cricket bat. He just felt comfortable with a thin handle. Duncan Fearnley made them specially, and Graeme's bats often used to break at the handle.

When Kerry Packer threw international cricket into chaos in 1977, Richards and fellow Springboks Eddie Barlow, Mike Proctor, Garth Le

Roux and Clive Rice were quick to join the rebel World Series Cricket.

Face Richards with a challenge, a key match, a television audience and he would rise to it. He plays himself in with clinical care, gradually unfolding his strokes until they flow all round the wicket. A perfect example was when Richards wound up the first WSC season by hitting up 101 not out for the Rest of the World against Australia at the Sydney Cricket Ground in the decisive Super-Test. There was no doubt that the title of the world's number one batsman lay between the South African dasher and Greg Chappell. Richards recalls:

> It wasn't a particularly good innings because by this stage I had gone over the top. I was 34 and the old mince pies were starting to go. It was for $100,000 winner-take-all, really big money in those days, and subconsciously I always needed such a challenge to produce the goods. People still say both teams shared the prize money, but I can tell you we got all of it.
>
> Ian Chappell came on when we needed two runs to win and promptly bowled four wides between Rod Marsh and square leg. Marshy was a bit upset about it, too.

In 1987 Richards became Natal's director of cricket, working from 8 am to 5 pm and sometimes even watering and rolling the Kingsmead pitch, which he would have sneered at doing in the past.

With wife Anne, originally from Perth, he and their two sons settled in Adelaide when he was appointed the South Australian Cricket Association's coach, but after a year Richards switched to Brisbane to take the job as chief executive of the Queensland Cricket Association.

SOUTH AUSTRALIA v WESTERN AUSTRALIA
Perth, 20–23 November 1970

South Australia

B.A. Richards lbw b Mann	356
J.J. Causby c Chadwick b Lock	38
I.M. Chappell st Marsh b Lock	129
G.S. Chappell c Marsh b McKenzie	11
K.G. Cunningham c Inverarity b Lock	13
K. Langley run out	7
E.W. Freeman c Irvine b Lock	6
R.P. Blundell b Mann	0
A.A. Mallett not out	6
T.J. Jenner c McKenzie b Mann	5
Sundries	4
	9 (dec) for 575

	O	M	R	W
McKenzie	19	2	101	1
Lillee	18	1	117	0
Brayshaw	12	1	69	0
Mann	20.6	1	120	3
Lock	16	1	108	4
Inverarity	8	0	56	0

Fall of wickets: 109, 417, 447, 551, 553, 563, 564, 575, 757

Western Australia

D. Chadwick c Blundell b Jenner	49	c and b Hammond	2
C. Scarff c Blundell b Hammond	11	b Cunningham	4
J.T. Irvine b Jenner	33	c an b G. Chappell	57
R.J. Inverarity c Chappell b Hammond	85	c and b G. Chappell	35
R.D. Meuleman retired hurt	28	absent injured	0
I.J. Brayshaw lbw b Freeman	22	c Richards b Mallett	13
R.W. Marsh c I. Chappell b Hammond	9	c I. Chappell b Richards	19
A.I. Mann c Blundell b Hammond	12	c I. Chappell b Hammond	1
D.K. Lillee c Cunningham b Hammond	12	b Hammond	6
G.D. McKenzie b Hammond	10	not out	18
G.A.R. Lock not out	2	c Hammond b Mallett	8
Sundries	26		9
	289		175

	O	M	R	W	O	M	R	W
Freeman	15	1	53	1	4	0	16	0
Hammond	12.3	1	54	6	9	2	25	3
G. Chappell	8	1	23	0	12	1	41	2
Jenner	22	4	78	2	8	0	25	0
Mallett	18	5	37	0	12.5	2	43	2
Cunningham	9	2	18	0	4	0	12	1
Richards					1	0	4	1

Fall of wickets
First innings: 33, 88, 110, 239, 256, 261, 270, 285, 289, 289
Second innings: 3, 15, 102, 110, 137, 141, 142, 161, 175, 175

DAVID HOOKES

David Hookes, who carved five successive fours off England skipper Tony Greig in the 1977 Centenary Test, puts one over the top.

DAVID HOOKES

When cocky young David Hookes smashed England skipper Tony Greig for five successive fours in the 1977 Centenary Test in Melbourne, Sir Donald Bradman said wistfully, 'For just five balls, I thought Frank Woolley had been reborn. As a lover of beautiful stroke-play, it did my heart good to see them.'

Such a comparison with England's legendary left-hander and the stature of the man who made it represented a stunning tribute to the 21-year-old rookie who had been thrust into the Test arena on the strength of four first class centuries for South Australia in only 11 days.

According to Hookes, Greig reacted with all the good grace of a bloodied heavyweight boxer, snarling in his clipped South African accent, 'Why don't you piss off?'

Hookes shot back, 'Better an Australian playing for Australia than a f- - - - - - Pommy import.'

Greig confronting an ego as big as his own? It was a frightening thought. According to Freddie Trueman, 'There's only one head bigger than Tony Greig's — and that's Birkenhead.'

That slashing innings of 56, with each of the five fours cheered almost hysterically as the 55,000 crowd saw a new young champion establishing himself, was the beginning of a roller coaster ride through big cricket. Along the way, Hookes was dropped from Australia's team four times, most recently in 1985 when he was vice-captain, and dumped as South Australian captain in 1990 following complaints from his senior players.

Recalling that famous clash with Greig, Hookes says:

> Before the Centenary Test, I'd had five 100s in six innings, so I felt pretty confident. My form was there. When I was out for 17 in the first innings, Greig sneered, 'He's just a school kid trying to play Test cricket.'
>
> Those five fours in a row? Well, every time I hit the ball it went for four. Another time I might play the same shot and a fieldsman would get it. My verbals with Greig were very much played up. It didn't bother me at all.

A search through the records revealed that such a feat was last achieved when Vic Richardson carved five successive fours from Johnny Douglas in the Melbourne Test of 1920–21.

Hookes suffered a terrible blow in 1978 when an Andy Roberts bouncer shattered his jaw and cheekbone in a World Series match at the Sydney Showground, and he explains:

> Subconsciously, it took me four or five years to get over it. I was in a very emotional state when the doctor in Sydney said it would take me five years to get over the mental scarring. He was probably right, but if he'd said six months, that would have been what it would have taken. That doctor has to take a lot of the blame.

Although he managed just a lone century in his 23 Tests, Hookes whipped up Australia's fastest first class century when he needed only 34 balls and 43 minutes to reach three figures for South Australia against Victoria, playing in Adelaide in the 1982–83 season. And in 1987 he joined forces with Wayne Phillips to figure in a Sheffield Shield record partnership of 462 (since surpassed by Steve and Mark Waugh) against Tasmania at his beloved Adelaide Oval. In that game, Hookes was unconquered with 306, smashing 41 fours and two sixes.

The popularity of Hookes in Adelaide is enormous because of the left-hander's willingness to attack the bowling with drives and cuts and take a chance in a bid to achieve an exciting finish. One of the world's most beautiful cricket grounds, Adelaide Oval is tailor-made for Hookes, with its short boundaries square of the wicket and a hard, true pitch which allows his sharp eye to compensate for his (at times) questionable technique. He mightn't follow the text book where foot placement is concerned, but who cares?

In Adelaide Hookes' fans claim he has been hard done by in the matter of Test caps. They point out that Steve Waugh at the start of his career played more Tests for less runs at a worse average than Hookes, yet never suffered the chop and recall treatment that Hookes had to put up with over an eight-year period. He says: 'My criticism of Bob Simpson is that he's always been quite public in suggesting I'm just an Adelaide Oval player. Gee, if you play half your games on one ground, I think that's an obvious statement.'

However, Hookes himself admits that he lacked the necessary qualities to be a consistent Test player. He made 1306 runs at a modest 34.36 in his 23 Tests, with his only Test century being 143 not out against minnows Sri Lanka. With typical bluntness, Hookes can quote five times when he had a Test century at his mercy only to throw his wicket away, either through an undisciplined shot or lack of composure.

'If I'd had a better grounding, or been a bit smarter,' he says, 'I would have converted two or three of them into centuries. The bottom line is that I didn't, so I wasn't a very good player at the Test level.'

The most glaring example occurred when he made 53 and 68 in the fourth Test of England's 1982–83 Ashes tour in Melbourne in a game

Australia lost by just three runs. That was by far his best Test series, as Hookes played in all five matches, making 344 runs at 49.14, but made four scores above 50 without once going on to three figures.

The *Australian*'s respected Terry Brindle sums up: 'Hookes' career remains an enigma. A young man who squandered the talent so unmistakable in his early halcyon days, or a wasted victim of a maverick relationship with authority.'

Nobody can quibble about Hookes' century off 34 balls at the Adelaide Oval in 1982. South Australia scored 409 in reply to Victoria's 260, with skipper Hookes hitting up 137. Graham Yallop closed Victoria's second innings at 9 for 420, leaving South Australia the seemingly impossible task of scoring 272 in approximately 30 overs. Over to Hookes.

> I was coming off a 50 and 80 in Brisbane, so I was in pretty good touch. My first innings century was one of the most satisfying innings technically I've ever played, I can't recall a single chance.
>
> Prior to the game, Yallop had said, 'We're here to play for a win.' Okay, fine. But he wasn't fair dinkum as he delayed closing the second innings until there were nine wickets down and we faced an impossible target. Still, I decided to open the innings and have a slog.
>
> Rick Darling faced the first over and only got a few, but I hit the first ball of King's over for six over mid-wicket. We took 16 or 17 off that over.
>
> I remember hitting a six onto the grandstand roof off Shaun Graf. After a while the only place they didn't have a man on the fence for Rod McCurdy was fine leg, so I stepped across and whipped two fours to that spot. They were the only two shots I premeditated.
>
> We raced to 100 in seven overs, but there was still another 170-odd runs needed plus the time factor. I got out for 107 going for a big slog. I'd got the century in 43 minutes off only 34 balls with three sixes and 17 fours, one of the three times I've made 100 in each innings of a match. It would have been quicker, too, if Yallop hadn't told McCurdy to take his boots off to waste some time.
>
> With wickets falling in the failing light, the chase was called off with six overs remaining and Victoria needing three wickets to win at 7 for 206. I had no idea I'd broken the record until I read it in the paper the next day.

There always has been an element of a rebel in this incorrigible fellow with a wicked wit who often speaks his mind compulsively. This has been costly at times: he was fined $1200 five years ago for suggesting Rod Marsh would make an excellent captain and that Kim Hughes could learn by serving an apprenticeship under him.

Controversy and Hookes have long gone hand in hand. In an extraordinary attack, Dr Ali Bacher, the managing director of the South African Cricket Union, said: 'We wanted Hookes as captain of the rebel team when he was Australia's vice-captain, but when it got down to crunch time he did not really appeal to us. His inclusion would have caused a major problem as he was not popular with the other chaps. I feel it must be because of the way he behaves.'

Hookes isn't the sort of man to mellow with age, and thank heavens for that. During his stint as South Australian captain he was savagely critical of the state of the Sydney and Melbourne wickets, the method of allocating Shield points and the honesty of NSW skipper Geoff Lawson. At the same time, Hookes led South Australia to a memorable victory in the 1981–82 Sheffield Shield.

When asked to pose for a shot with West Indian import Joel Garner when South Australia practised in the Sydney Cricket Ground nets, Hookes called: 'Hey Bird, the press wants a black and white shot.' Garner gave a deep chuckle.

The *Australian*'s Malcolm Conn tells of another occasion on which Hookes was criticised for not bowling West Indian-born Gladstone Small more in a game against New Zealand. 'Look mate,' said Hookes, 'we have an agreement here that I don't bowl the black feller until the temperature gets over 110 degrees.'

Like Garner, Small was alongside Hookes and enjoyed the joke. Hookes then told him to remember his place, carry the captain's bag and walk three paces behind him. But one wonders what the Racial Discrimination people might have made of Hookes if the story was told maliciously or out of context.

Recalling his record partnership of 462 with Wayne Phillips against Tasmania in which Hookes finished with 306 not out, he says:

> It wasn't a destructive innings because I only hit two sixes. Wayne and I went on and on and seemed to score off every ball. We put on 188 in one session and it only felt like 100. Tasmania got 240, and although this sounds stupid, they bowled quite well. They stuck at it all day on a very good pitch. A typical Adelaide pitch. I didn't give a chance and Wayne only gave one.
>
> We could have gone on and broken all the world records, but I wouldn't have been able to live with myself if I'd batted on and Tasmania finished the last day with nine wickets down and a draw.

In 1983 Hookes was offered a fortune to switch to Victoria, but changed his mind at the last moment after originally deciding to make the jump.

He explains: 'I was going to fly over and sign, but a couple of things came up in the next 24 hours that kept me in Adelaide. For one thing, the Premier, John Bannon, got involved.'

So Victoria continued to suffer from Hookes' flashing blade. In February 1989 he shrugged off a painful blow from Merv Hughes to whip up 133 in Melbourne, the eighth time he'd scored a century in a session and the fourth time he'd achieved this feat against Victoria.

Early in his career Hookes received some help from Sir Donald Bradman, but he rarely sees him these days. He says: 'I sit next to him at SACA functions, but that's all. In the early days he'd spend a bit of time with me, though. We'd talk about the way I'd play a particular shot. When Bradman says something, you take notice of it.'

Hookes himself found an unusual solution after being turned inside out by Pakistan's slow bowlers, scoring a mere ten runs in six innings when Australia toured there in 1979. Finally the penny dropped that the way to play spin wasn't just with his pads. Hookes painfully recalls, 'It was pad, pad, pad and usually out, out, out. I might as well have gone in without a bat.'

After returning home, he recruited former Test off spinner Ashley Mallett to bowl to him in the nets in workouts during which Hookes wore no pads. It cost him plenty of lumps on the shins and knees, but got the desired results.

Perhaps the greatest irony of his career came when Hookes was dropped from the Australian team for the last time in 1985. A week later he carved 243 from 256 balls with ten sixes and 26 fours against NSW in Adelaide, with Test selector Greg Chappell sitting in the stand.

Hookes, quite rightly, didn't think he was out of form when dropped after a Test win over New Zealand in Sydney in which he played a key role in the run chase. He figured in a 66 partnership with Greg Matthews in only 40 minutes. With not a clue that vice-captain Hookes was facing the chop, skipper Allan Border said: 'The vice-captain was sensational this afternoon. Throughout the game he has been a tower of strength to me as far as making decisions went. It was very pleasing for me to have him play so well at the end. It hopefully means we can build up some sort of partnership with the long-term thing in mind.'

At the start of the season Greg Chappell had impressed on Hookes the need to play long, responsible innings rather than the brief, explosive ones for which he was famous. For a while Hookes played sadly out of character, with a three-hour century against the New Zealanders regaining him a Test spot at the age of 30. However, hours hunched over a bat was not the real Hookes. After his savagely struck 243, Hookes said: 'I've been stuffing around a bit too much recently. Today I played it my way.'

Typically, Hookes goes for a couple of team achievements as his most satisfying moments in cricket. He says:

> Winning the last four matches outright to grab the Sheffield Shield in 1981–82. The celebrations went on for 48 hours. When we were chasing a target in the last game against Victoria in Adelaide, people were parking up in King William Street and running down the hill to the ground. There must have been 10,000 there at five o'clock.
>
> Regaining the Ashes in 1982–83 was another highlight because in England in 1977 we'd lost 3–0. I've enjoyed a lot of partnerships with Darren Lehmann because he plays so well. I got a good 100 in 1989–90 against Tasmania in Devonport on a very bad pitch on which David Gilbert got seven wickets. I batted for a long, long time.

Now a sports presenter with radio 5AA, Hookes was shocked and deeply wounded when he lost the South Australian captaincy after leading his State in 90 first class matches, more than anyone except Les Favell. He explains:

> Having a job I'd had for 10 years taken away in the manner it was really hurt, particularly as I was told after other people had been told. It came right out of the blue, and it'll take a few years to find out the full facts. In the selectors' defence, they are entitled to make any decision they want. It probably warranted being done a little bit differently, given that there's only been five State cricket captains in this town in such a long time — Bradman, Ridings, Favell, Chappell and Hookes.

However, Hookes shrugged off his disappointment and a first innings duck to hit a slashing 195 against Queensland in Brisbane in the opening game of the 1990–91 Shield season. It was his 27th first class century for South Australia, one better than Ian Chappell's record.

And when Hookes carved 178 runs with five sixes and 21 fours from Queensland's attack in the return game in Adelaide, he swept past Les Favell's record of 9556 first class runs for the State. At 35, there obviously were a lot more runs going to flow from his dashing bat.

SOUTH AUSTRALIA v VICTORIA
Adelaide, 22–25 October 1982

Victoria

J.M. Wiener c Hookes b Garner	2	b Garner	73
G.M. Watts c Hilditch b Garner	0	c Wright b Hogg	0
G.N. Yallop c Darling b Sincock	28	c and b Sincock	151
P.J. Davies c Garner b Hookes	29	b Garner	27
B.C. Green c Wright b Garner	14	c Harris b Inverarity	70
P.J. Cox c Hogg by Garner	20	c and b Harms	47
S.F. Graf c Garner b Harms	48	c Wright b Inverarity	18
P.G. Sacristanti c Garner b Sincock	55	lbw b Harms	2
P.D. Wright b Hogg	54	not out	15
R.J. McCurdy not out	5	lbw b Inverarity	9
J.D. Higgs b Hogg	0	not out	1
Sundries	5		7
	260		9 (dec) for 420

	O	M	R	W	O	M	R	W
Garner	28	5	73	4			81	2
Hogg	20.1	4	38	2	21	6	62	1
Sincock	18	9	50	2	18	3	77	1
Harms	14	4	38	1	29	9	71	2
Hookes	3	1	8	1	2	1	6	0
Inverarity	14	5	48	0	41	7	116	3

Fall of wickets
First innings: 1, 2, 39, 63, 95, 109, 168, 248, 256, 260
Second innings: 0, 141, 220, 261, 373, 380, 404, 418

South Australia

W.M. Darling c McCurdy b King	10	c Sacristani b McCurdy	11
K.P. Harris c Sacristani b McCurdy	9	(8) lbw b Graf	0
A.M.J. Hilditch c Graf	42	(9) not out	0
R.J. Inverarity lbw McCurdy	126	(7) not out	0
D.W. Hookes c Sacristani b Cox	137	(2) c Green b McCurdy	107
R.J. Zadow c Wiener b King	5	lbw b McCurdy	8
K.J. Wright c Davies b King	33	(3) b McCurdy	30
C.L. Harms c Wiener b Green	21	(5) c Sacristani b McCurdy	3
J. Garner c Sacristani b King	7	(4) b Graf	19
R.M. Hogg c Wiener b King	0		
A.J. Sincock not out	8		
Sundries	11		13
	409		7 for 206

	O	M	R	W	O	M	R	W
McCurdy	23	2	95	2	12	0	88	5
King	28	5	88	5	2	0	38	0
Graf	23	5	74	1	10	0	67	2
Cox	25	3	69	1				
Higgs	10	1	46	0				
Green	4.3	1	16	1				
Yallop	5	2	10	0				

Fall of wickets
First innings: 16, 28, 76, 288, 301, 367, 383, 386, 390, 409
Second innings: 122, 128, 154, 159, 184, 203, 204

Match drawn

ALLAN BORDER

Allan Border, who has scored more Test runs, held more Test catches and played more Tests than any other Australian.

ALLAN BORDER

'Allan Border has not so much style as modus operandi. He is utterly practical.' John Woodcock, *The Times.*

When Allan Border dies, the inscription on his gravestone should say simply, 'He was at his best when the chips were down'. With an icy look and stubble on his chin, AB has shored up the Australian innings so many times with a counter attack that it has become his trademark.

The London *Observer* comments: 'Border is never prepared to say die — except when calling himself a dinky-di Aussie.' Defiant and gritty, left-hander Border has scored more Test runs, taken more Test catches and played more Tests than any other Australian, averaging more than 50 runs per innings at the time of writing. His list of Test centuries is so long that it looks like the itinerary of the world's most popular rock band.

As a cricketer with more than 9000 Test runs in his portfolio, he has earned the epithet of great, yet Border says modestly: 'I just play a couple of shots [principally the cut and drive] reasonably well and then become hard to get out.' With total sincerity, he adds, 'If you play enough games, you will pass these milestones.' Utter nonsense, of course, but evidence why Border is held in universal admiration by his peers.

Border always has had the capacity to build an innings. His 22nd Test century, when he defied stifling heat and scored 205 against New Zealand in Adelaide in 1987, was his seventh of more than 150; on another seven occasions he has been unconquered between 100 and 150. This was the innings in which he went past Greg Chappell and Sir Donald Bradman as Australia's greatest Test run-getter, but he was adamant he couldn't be compared to Chappell and no one could be compared to Sir Donald.

With a whiplash left arm developed by baseball, Border has made direct hits on the stumps to run out countless Test rivals, while his innocent-looking spinners once gave him a six for 46 Test haul against the West Indies at the Sydney Cricket Ground, including the prize wicket of Viv Richards.

At 5ft 9in (175 cm) and 12 stone (76 kg) Border typifies the little Aussie battler, so he was a popular choice as Australian of the Year in 1989 after leading Australia to a 4–0 Ashes triumph in England. A year later he was awarded the Order of Australia.

Border travels well, too, as 12 of his 23 Test centuries have been scored on foreign soil. They love this affable fellow in the West Indies and he is a hero to the millions of cricket devotees in India and Pakistan.

The son of a wool broker, Allan Robert Border was born on 27 July 1955 in Sydney, where he grew up in a house opposite Mosman Oval. For a while he preferred baseball to cricket, and it was of this period that he says: 'I went through a stage where I didn't give a hoot about cricket or anything else. I wanted to lie on the beach or bum around for a while.'

It was Barry Knight, the former England player, who lured him back to cricket when he became coach of Mosman, the club of the famed Stan McCabe and former Australian captain Ian Craig. Before long Border was playing for NSW and he was hoisted into Test cricket when Kerry Packer's chequebook lured the leading Australian players to the breakaway World Series Cricket.

When the split was healed, Border soon was in the new-look Australian side alongside the brothers Chappell, Dennis Lillee and Rod Marsh. He moulded himself, in particular, on Ian Chappell, and cultivated the same tough, unyielding image. Like Chappell, he used not to shave during a five-day Test. Like Chappell, he is fiercely loyal to his players.

Soon Border transferred from his native NSW to Queensland, agreeing to move soon after his marriage to Jane in 1980. It was a move that led to him suddenly and begrudgingly being thrust into the Australian captaincy in 1984 when Kim Hughes, unable to cope with the pressure and the press, sobbed his way from centre stage after the Second Test against the West Indies.

Border is the epitome of the modern jet-set sportsman, spending most of his life on the circuit in hotel, ground and airport, playing cricket all through the year and all around the globe and being highly paid to do so.

The day I chatted with Border at the Sydney Cricket Ground, he gave a fairly convincing impression of being a prisoner in a privileged world as he prepared for the first of the 1991 one-day finals against New Zealand.

After batting and bowling in the nets, Border comfortably gave TV interviews for home and New Zealand consumption and then had a talk with the waiting media writers. He spoke guardedly about the next day's game, becoming brief and monosyllabic at the hint of anything controversial. But his eyes sparkled at the mention of a 78 he had shot at Royal Melbourne golf course the previous day to take the money off Geoff Marsh and Dean Jones.

Then it was off to fielding practice, followed by physio treatment for a groin injury that was to prevent him playing the next day, and a radio interview. Border apologised for keeping me waiting, but he needn't have bothered. Beside the duties of an Australian cricket captain, wrestling an octopus would seem easy.

Asked to nominate his finest century, Border unhesitatingly chose his double of 98 not out and 100 not out against the West Indies in Port-of-Spain, Trinidad, in 1984 as the finest batting of his life. On that trip, his training schedule included skipping and running up and down stairs to ensure he was light on his feet. With the pitch green and damp, the Windies omitted spinner Roger Harper and brought in an extra fast man, Milton Small, to support Joel Garner, Malcolm Marshall and Wayne Daniel. Standing in for injured skipper Clive Lloyd, Viv Richards won the toss and unhesitatingly invited the Australians to bat.

Ignored for a recent tour of India and hearing talk that he was over the hill, rubber-limbed, sky-scraping Garner charged in with a point to prove. With his outrageous, steepling bounce from the pitch, he was almost unplayable. Garner whipped out Kepler Wessels, Wayne Phillips and Greg Ritchie to have Australia rocking at 3 for 16 when Border, unsmiling and moustache pouting with defiant trim, came to the crease. He recalls:

> We were in all sorts of strife, but I batted as well as you can bat against that sort of bowling on that sort of wicket. Joel Garner was awesome. For some years he had been used by the Windies more as a stock bowler — medium-fast, but with an incredible bounce. Now Garner had become a genuine fast bowler, rushing in and bowling quite swiftly. This was one of the games where he really hit his straps. They gave the new ball to big Joel and he got stuck into us.
>
> When I first struck Garner, it came as a complete shock to the system. He made me feel totally out of my depth — I just couldn't pick up his length and middle the ball. As he delivered the ball from such a great height, every delivery looked like it was going to be a bouncer. For a while Joel gave me more trouble than any bowler I've faced, and it really did spur me on to succeed in Test cricket. Playing so much cricket against the Windies in the early 1980s, I gradually adjusted to it — if you can ever get used to that sort of bowling. Over the years the Big Bird and I have had some pretty good contests.
>
> Although he enjoyed the battle, Garner never had much to say out on the field and neither did the other West Indian players, unlike the current Australian fast bowlers. This has crept into our game over the last few years, and I don't mind as long as it's reasonably sensible. Not too over the top.

By the time rain brought a merciful halt to the first day's play, Australia was reeling at 4 for 55, with Garner having grabbed all four wickets at a cost of 22 runs off eight devilish overs. This sort of bowling caused England skipper Mike Brearley to ask Lord's if they could heighten the sightboard at the Nursery end because the ball was being lost in the trees of London Zoo when Garner bowled.

With help from David Hookes and Dean Jones, Border got to 92 when rain again intruded, cutting short the second day. It was a gutsy effort as he had to shrug off dry-retching caused by a stomach upset. Several times the ball was a blur of red as it catapulted from the pitch to smash into Border's ribs or hit him over the heart. When last man Terry Alderman came in the next morning, Border had reached 98. Garner promptly delivered Allan a magnificent over, with each ball spitting menace as it leapt from the pitch. He was unable to nudge a run from them, and was left unconquered with 98 when Alderman was caught at slip off a bumper. Australia was out for 255 and Garner finished with 6 for 60.

With six hours' play lost on the first two days, Richards declared the West Indies innings at 8 for 468 with a lead of 213 after Jeff Dujon hit up 130 and Gus Logie 97 in a spectacular sixth wicket stand. Once again Australia started badly and were 4 for 114 with five hours left for play when Border took block. It was 5 for 115 when night watchman Tom Hogan departed the scene. Border recalls:

> I made up my mind that if I was going to join the procession back to the pavilion, it was going to be after a fight. The wicket was playing pretty well by this stage, and Joel Garner was struggling with a tummy upset. He'd bowl a spell and have to leave the field and then come back. One of those sort of days.
>
> I was batting particularly well, but when Rodney Hogg came in at 8 for 196 and three hours left to be played, we were in a position comparable with Custer and his Seventh Cavalry at Little Bighorn.
>
> Hoggy hung around for an hour, but when Viv Richards got him just after tea we were 25 runs ahead with last man Terry Alderman coming out and 105 minutes remaining. No disrespect to Terry, but I didn't think we had a hope of playing out time.
>
> 'We'll give it our best shot,' I told him. 'If we can bat for an hour, we can get out of it. We'll pick up whatever runs we can because that'll make it harder for them to win.' Like Hoggy, Terry really gutsed it out, and we managed to get through the second new ball. When Richards came back with spin, Terry prodded forward. He was batting very, very well and I was scoring runs.
>
> With four overs left, it was obvious we'd saved the game. Richards tossed

> the ball to Gus Logie, I hit the four I needed for my 100 and Viv strolled over, shook hands and called the game off with 3.5 overs left. It was a nice gesture by Viv to give me a chance of completing my century by continuing even though the Windies didn't have half a sniff of winning.
>
> Terry finished with 21 not out, and to my delight the crowd gave us a standing ovation as we left the field. West Indians are fiercely parochial and regard the other team as villains, the enemy. Yet here they were greeting us like home-town heroes. It was quite moving.

In a match in which none of his Australian colleagues could manage a half century, Border had batted for ten and a half hours, faced 535 mainly hostile deliveries under the fiercest of pressure and finished with 198 defiant runs without being dismissed. Winston Churchill would have been proud of him.

It revived memories of Border's epic last wicket stand with Jeff Thomson against England in Melbourne's amphitheatre of concrete skyscrapers, when they kept the nation on tenterhooks by scoring 74 nail-biting runs before Thomson was out three runs short of the target. Looking back to the West Indies Test, Border recalls:

> Considering the attack we faced and the wicket we played on, the combined effort of scoring 98 not out and 100 not out was as good as I've ever played. No particular shots stand out because I got into a certain routine. Cut shots, cover drives, a lot of ducking and diving. I got hit a couple of times, but I was in pretty good nick and playing well. In a normal innings against the Windies, you always wear a couple.
>
> Their major weapon is that they've got four fast bowlers who bowl a lot of bouncers and short pitched balls to keep you under pressure. When they saw I was playing reasonably well at Port-of-Spain, they didn't bounce me as much as the others. In the first innings I largely got out of the way, but in the second knock I had a bit of a hook and got away with it.
>
> The first innings was the better effort because the conditions then were downright dangerous. The wicket was damp, Joel Garner was ferocious and Australia was in deep trouble. By the second innings the wicket had dried out and Garner, their main strike bowler, was off the field crook.

Not far behind that heroic performance at Port-of-Spain, Border puts his 196 at Lord's in 1985, a knock which set up an Australian victory by four wickets which squared the series. In the second innings, he saw Australia home with an undefeated 41. Border recalls:

This was probably as good an innings as I've put together, and I counted that 100 pretty special for three reasons: it was against England at Lord's, which is one of my favourite grounds; it was a big 100; and we won the Test match. It's all the more enjoyable when you've made a big contribution towards winning. When you leave the dressing room and walk down through the Long Room to take the field, the history of the place just hits you. It's phenomenal, and no other ground can match it.

Because the wicket looked to have a little juice in it, I put England in after winning the toss and with Craig McDermott taking six wickets, we bowled them out for 290. I was just short of my 100 when bad light stopped play on the second day and went on to 196 as we got 425. The wicket was starting to wear, and when leg spinner Bob Holland snared five wickets in their second dig, we were left with 127 to win.

When I came in at 3 for 22, Ian Botham, who was supposed to be a mate of mine, strolled past singing, 'Remember 81, remember 81.' I got the message. Needing only 130 to win, we had been skittled for 111 in the third Test at Leeds that year after Ian himself had smashed us for 149 runs. Well, this just made me determined there wouldn't be another fiasco and I was there at the finish, when Simon O'Donnell made the winning hit.

With an unerring eye for dispatching the bad ball and superb footwork, particularly to the spinners, Border has had many, many other great innings with his 2lb 10oz bat.

For instance, Greg Chappell says Border's Test double of 150 not out and 153 against Pakistan in 1979–80 will live long in his memory, with the slow men seemingly serving up a ball as big as a watermelon to him. Border also competed a century in each innings against New Zealand with 140 and 114 not out in Christchurch in 1985–86.

When Border comes to the wicket in a crisis, he'll lay ball after ball dead at his feet. With the red blob in the centre of his bat getting larger and larger, he'll begin to cut with a snap, drive crisply and whip the ball to leg with the sureness of touch of a chef tossing a pizza.

Those who pigeonhole Border as a gutsy, limpet-batted plugger should heed the Nehru Cup in India in 1989 in which the Australian skipper carved 84 off England in only 44 balls, his five sixes including three off successive balls from fast man Gladstone Small. Recalling such flashing, dashing, slashing play with relish, Border says:

It was one of those freak days where I hit everything in the middle of the bat. We'd struggled on a difficult wicket and at the 43rd over were only 140-odd. That's when I started the onslaught.

> I don't think I have ever struck the ball so hard. When I hit the three sixes off Small, he wasn't trying to bounce me. He was pushing the ball up into the blockhole so I couldn't get up and under him, but left it a bit short. I was swinging the bat and collected all three balls so sweetly that each one of them went out of the ground.

When Ernest Hemingway lost the ability to write, he woke up one morning and shot himself. However, when Border's Test cricket career is over, he'll happily spend most of his time with wife Jane and children Nicole and Dene in Brisbane, where he'll play as much golf as possible and tend to the vast gardens surrounding his lovely home in upper middle-class suburbia. No doubt the TV commentary box beckons.

When he first took over the Australian captaincy, Border inherited a bad team and scowled his way through three losing years in which he carried the side with his batting. In those days the definition of an optimist was an Australian opener who bothered to put zinc cream on his nose.

Captain Grumpy, some of the Australian players called him, and several times Border threatened to resign from the job. With Allan developing into an astute and innovative leader, the Australians suddenly caught fire and won the 1987 World Cup in India as an aperitif to a stunning 4–0 Ashes triumph in England.

Oddly enough, when the Australian team came good Border's century-habit promptly deserted him. He continued to score consistently, but he went two years without a Test century. He admitted: 'I am not quite as gritty and determined as I have been in the past. I have probably relaxed to an extent in my own mind because the other fellows are playing so well and the team is doing so well. Maybe I have let my game go a bit because we have become successful.'

When he finally quits the game with a mountain of Test runs, more than anything Allan Border will be remembered as a man who somehow seemed to breathe slower when everyone else was breathing fast. A man who was at his best when the chips were down.

ALLAN BORDER'S TEST TONS

105	v Pakistan, Melbourne 1978–79
162	v India, Madras 1979–80
115	v England, Perth 1979–80
150 not out	v Pakistan, Lahore 1979–80
153	v Pakistan, Lahore 1979–80
124	v India, Melbourne 1980–81
123 not out	v England, Manchester 1981
106 not out	v England, The Oval 1981
126	v West Indies, Adelaide 1981–82
118	v Pakistan, Brisbane 1983–84
117	v Pakistan, Adelaide 1983–84
100 not out	v West Indies, Port-of-Spain 1984
196	v England, Lord's 1985
146 not out	v England, Manchester 1985
152 not out	v New Zealand, Brisbane 1985–86
163	v India, Melbourne 1985–86
140	v New Zealand, Christchurch 1986
114 not out	v New Zealand, Christchurch 1986
106	v India, Madras 1986–87
125	v England, Perth 1986–87
100 not out	v England, Adelaide 1986–87
205	v New Zealand, Adelaide 1987–88
113 not out	v Pakistan, Faisalabad 1988–89

AUSTRALIA v WEST INDIES
Port-of-Spain, 16–21 March 1984

Australia

K.C. Wessels c Gomes b Garner	4	lbw b Garner 8
W.B. Phillips c Dujon b Garner	4	run out 0
G.M. Ritchie b Garner	1	b Small 26
K.J. Hughes c Dujon b Garner	24	lbw b Marshall 33
A.R. Border not out	98	(6) not out 100
D.W. Hookes b Garner	23	(7) c Richardson b Gomes 21
D.M. Jones c and b Richards	48	(8) b Richards 5
G.F. Lawson c and b Daniel	14	(9) b Marshall 20
T.G. Hogan c Greenidge b Daniel	0	(5) c Logie b Daniel 38
R.M. Hogg c Marshall b Daniel	11	c Garner b Richards 9
T.M. Alderman c Richardson b Garner	1	not out 21
Sundries	27	22
	255	9 for 299

	O	M	R	W	O	M	R	W
Garner	28.1	9	60	6	15	4	35	1
Marshall	19	4	73	0	22	3	73	2
Daniel	15	2	40	3	9	3	11	1
Small	10	3	24	0	14	2	51	1
Gomes	10	0	33	0	27	5	53	1
Richards	10	4	15	1	25	5	65	2
Logie					0.1	0	4	0

Fall of wickets
First innings: 4, 7, 16, 50, 85, 185, 233, 233, 253, 255
Second innings: 1, 35, 41, 114, 115, 153, 162, 196, 238

West Indies

C.G. Greenidge c Phillips b Hogg	24
D.L. Haynes run out	53
R.B. Richardson c Wessels b Alderman	23
I.V.A. Richards c Phillips b Alderman	76
H.A. Gomes b Lawson	3
A.I. Logie lbw b Hogan	97
P.J.L. Dujon b Hogan	130
M.D. Marshall lbw b Lawson	10
J. Garner not out	24
W.W. Daniel not out	6
Sundries	22
	8 (dec) for 468

	O	M	R	W
Lawson	32	3	132	2
Hogg	31	2	103	1
Alderman	35	9	91	2
Hogan	28	3	123	2

Fall of wickets: 35, 93, 124, 129, 229, 387, 430, 462

Match drawn

DENISE ANNETTS AND LINDSAY REELER

Lindsay Reeler (left), seen here in watchful mood, averaged a stunning 149.33 when Australia won the 1988 World Cup; Denise Annetts (right) shows the style that made her a world record-holder.

DENISE ANNETTS AND LINDSAY REELER

'We've always set the trend. Remember women cricketers were the first to bowl overarm.' Rachel Heyhoe Flint (former captain of the England team)

Even though Australia's women cricketers are the world champions, much of that success has stayed the secret of the initiated few, with Denise Annetts and Lindsay Reeler remaining two of the unsung heroines of Australian sport. Apart from the 5000 to 6000 women who play cricket in Australia, how many people know that Annetts, a Sydney pharmacist who stands only 5 ft $\frac{3}{4}$ in (154 cm), became the world record-holder when she whipped up 193 run out in the second Test against England at Collingham, Yorkshire, in August 1987 when she was 23 years old.

In that innings she figured in a world record partnership of 309 with Zambian-born Reeler, whose 110 not out was the world's slowest Test century by a woman. Reeler's opening partner in that game was Denise Emerson, always labelled as the sister of Australian pace bowler Terry Alderman. Denise and Terry were immortalised by TV commentator Tony Cozier with the breathless words, 'This is the first time, I believe, that a brother and sister of different sexes have played for Australia at the same time.'

A year later at the Melbourne Cricket Ground, Lyn Larsen's Australian team completed a hat trick of victories in the World Cup, with Reeler's stylish strokes giving her a stunning average of 149.33 per innings in spite of a duck.

And who was the first cricketer in the world to capture the all-rounder's double of ten wickets and 100 runs in a Test? Statisticians give credit to Alan Davidson for his triumph against the West Indies in the stupendous tied Test in Brisbane in 1960. Wrong — it was Australia's Betty Wilson, who snared 7 for 7 including a hat trick on a first day sticky, hit up exactly 100 in the second innings, then grabbed a further 4 for 9 in a Test against England at St Kilda, Melbourne, in February 1958.

If one of Allan Border's men had achieved any of these records, he would never be off the front pages. But Denise and Lindsay continue to be shunned by most of the media in spite of their superlative skills.

There's nothing new about women playing cricket. In fact, Christina Willes is credited with inventing overarm bowling way back in 1822.

Finding that the voluminous skirts of the period impeded her bowling underarm to give her brother John batting practice while he was convalescing after an illness, Christina bowled him out with an over-the-shoulder delivery.

Willes, Kentish squire and patron of all manly sports, was so struck by her success that he forthwith adopted the style himself. However, when he tried this method for Kent against the Marylebone Cricket Club (MCC) at Lord's, he was immediately no-balled for bowling his new-fangled stuff. Willes threw down the ball, jumped on his horse and rode out of Lord's, vowing he would never play again. Nor did he, though his sister's invention was made law six years later by the MCC, cricket's governing body.

It was a shame he chose to quit the game, as supporters extravagantly claimed that Willes, his sister and his dog could beat any eleven in England.

To the dismay of the feminists, it was squire John who got the glory from his sister's innovation, and his tombstone stands engraved for all to see — 'He was the first to introduce round-arm bowling into cricket.'

According to the Melbourne *Argus*, the first women's cricket match in Australia was played at Bendigo in 1874. (An earlier game was played, in 1855, but no scores survived.)

The account of the first organised women's match in Australia was recorded for posterity by the May 1886 issue of *Cricket,* which reported:

> There was considerably over a thousand persons at the Sydney Association Ground on Monday afternoon, the majority of those present being ladies. The two elevens were called the Siroccos and Fernleas respectively, the former wearing a cardinal and blue costume, while the latter were attired in black and gold. They began at 2 pm and continued until half past six, with the Burwood band playing selections during the afternoon. Miss Louisa Gregory captained the wearers of yellow and black, while her sister Nellie led on the amazons of the scarlet and blue.
>
> The palm for all-round cricket must be awarded to Miss R. Deane, who displayed such excellence in all departments of the game that many players in our senior clubs would envy. The Misses Gregory and Englestoff also shone to great advantage, evincing a thorough knowledge of the intricacies of the game. The wicketkeepers Miss L. Gregory and Jeffreys were very smart behind the sticks, and at times fairly brought the house down with their dexterity. The fielding was generally good, but the ladies with several exceptions could not throw. Their bowling was mostly round-arm, the obsolete grubber being resorted to only by one bowler.

Rosalie Deane was to achieve lasting fame as the first scorer of a century in each innings. She accomplished this feat in Sydney in 1891, making 195 and 104 for the Intercolonial Ladies Club against the Sydney club.

A hundred years ago, the Victorian concept of women obliged them to wilt genteely in unhygienic and constricting clothes. Physical exertion was discouraged; indeed, the garments of the period would scarcely permit it. Now tennis courts are thronged with the bare, brown legs of girls whose skirts grow shorter and shorter. Girls swim and ski, girls ride surfboards, girls run and play golf, basketball, hockey and cricket. Sure, there are plenty of mountainous sports girls clumping about, but what about Florence Griffith-Joyner, the very embodiment of grace, a beautiful, flowing, lissom sight as she bounded over the track at the Seoul Olympics.

Our women cricketers can't be accused of lacking femininity, either. They look so cool and crisp in their divided skirts, long socks and baggy green caps. Today's Australian players are light years distant in looks and style from when the first women's Test was played in Brisbane in December 1934, with Betty Archdale's touring English team winning by nine wickets. Six-ball overs and a lighter five-ounce (1.4 kg) ball were innovations adopted during that trip.

When the 1987 Australian team played a one-day match at Lord's, MCC president Colin Cowdrey said, 'I hope to see women here again, certainly England and Australia. These two always should play here.'

The man who played 11 times for England added, 'The standard was very good. I was especially impressed with the fielding, and the batting of the Australian openers [Reeler and Emerson] was worth seeing, particularly their cover-driving.'

If iron-fisted discipline counts for anything, it was no surprise when the first Australian women's team to tour England in 1937 won the first Test played there by 31 runs at Northampton. Led by NSW's Margaret Peden, the tourists were allowed scant opportunity for social licence during the trip as the rules laid down by the Australian Women's Cricket Association ordained that:

- No member shall drink, smoke or gamble while on tour.
- No girl may be accompanied by her husband, a relation or a friend.
- Writing articles on cricket during the tour is strictly forbidden.
- While on board ship, no girl shall visit the top deck of the liner after dinner.
- Members of the team must retire to bed by 10 pm during the voyage and will do physical drill at 7.15 am daily except Sundays.

When Denise Annetts played at Lord's in 1987, the TV commentators drily described her as being 'some way short of Joel Garner in height'. When quizzed about her height, Denise firmly insists that she is 'five feet and three quarters of an inch,' which sounds a mite better than the metric equivalent.

Noted for her fast-moving, aggressive method, Annetts was in love with cricket from the time she spent six hours a day glued to the TV set when she was only six years old and the Tests were on. 'Even before he became popular, Allan Border was my favourite player,' she says. 'He concentrates and is very much a placement player like myself.'

Soon Denise was playing cricket with her four brothers, a perfect grounding for her schoolday sport at Abbotsleigh on Sydney's leafy North Shore where she was coached by Kit Raymond, a former Australian wicketkeeper. When Annetts was 16, her pharmacist father Neville Annetts gave Denise a Gray Nicolls scoop bat. She says, 'It was very heavy, full-sized and quite long, but I learned to bat with it. Now I can't use too light a bat. The weight gives extra power to my shots.'

At 21 and having played hockey for NSW for four years, Annetts was invited to the Australian Institute of Sport in Canberra. It had become impossible to combine the two sports, so Denise chose cricket, partly because the daily AIS training program would leave her little time for anything else. When time allows, however, she still plays hockey for the Mirrabooka club in Sydney.

Reviewing Denise's world record 193 in six and a quarter hours against England at Collingham in 1987, *Wisden* (the bible of cricket) said, 'She batted beautifully, her innings full of memorable cuts, leg glides and pulls through mid-wicket on a pitch that was soft, very slow and turned appreciably throughout.' Recalling the innings that made her NSW Sportswoman of the Year, Annetts said:

> Once in everyone's career it happens, I suppose. It was just so easy to score runs and there were no chances. I felt I could do anything. Put every ball where I wanted to. After England were out for 201, I came in at 2 for 37 and started fairly slowly, but soon I got on top of the bowling. It kept raining on and off and there was one interruption after another during my innings, but I was very much in form.
>
> Collingham is quite a large ground, but I managed 30 fours. I've got a one-day pull shot, but in Tests I'm mainly a driver and my fours coming from finding the gaps rather than lofting shots. Although I've got a solid little body, I get my runs from timing rather than hitting the ball hard.
>
> Because I'm small, I don't get a lot of runs with back-foot drives. Yet when

a young girl came on to bowl for England, I hit her for three or four fours in a row off the back foot.

Lindsay hadn't got a century in a Test before, so she tended to play a sheet anchor role. We're good friends and that helps us bat well together. Everyone says how magnificent Lindsay's shots are, so I'm just happy to be the one at the other end scoring the little ones.

Getting run out for 193 was a good lesson about wearing spikes. I thought I'd hit a ball past an English fielder and took off. Lindsay quite rightly said no, and I slipped trying to get back. I wear spikes now, though. As I have very small feet, I have to get them specially made. I went in at 12.28 on the second day and faced 365 balls before getting out at 2.16 pm the next day.

As we'd won the first Test, we didn't close the innings until 3 for 346 to ensure we couldn't lose. Another draw in the third Test marked the first series loss at home for England since international games for women began in 1934.

Annetts (48 not out) and Reeler (59 not out) figured in an unfinished stand of 115 when Australia got 2 for 129 in reply to England's 7 for 127 off 60 overs in the 1988 World Cup final at the Melbourne Cricket Ground. To help identify the players, the girls wore numbers on their backs.

Women's cricket draws crowds of up to 30,000 in India. Annetts says: 'The West Indies play women's cricket, too, but they're very poor and have no money to tour. They're wild and woolly like the West Indies men's team used to be. Very fast bowlers and big hitters who don't wear gloves when they're batting.'

How good are Australia's women cricketers? 'I've only played women's cricket, so I don't really know,' Denise says. 'If I'd started out in men's cricket and stuck with it, it's possible I could have played first grade. I've batted against guys in the nets without any real trouble, but I've not faced real pace. Karen Price played A grade men's cricket with West Pennant Hills in Sydney and won the bowling average. Still, you don't see Martina Navratilova playing John McEnroe.'

Lindsay Reeler doesn't agree with suggestions that her upright, classical stroke-play would enable her to play in a men's first grade team. She explains:

I've practised a lot with first grade guys in the nets, and I can hold my own when they pitch the ball up. But if they drop it short, a woman would be in trouble. Even if a woman could hit the pitch hard enough to bowl bouncers, it would be frowned upon. Men bowl faster, swing the ball more and run much quicker in the field.

> We just don't have the power of men, but women are women. They make up half the world's population. They have abilities, talents and strengths.

Reeler's most satisfying century is the snail's pace 110 not out she compiled in 440 minutes while Annetts was busily scoring 193 in their world record partnership of 309 against England in 1987. She explains:

> I was really happy with it because I batted very much out of character. I wasn't batting well, but managed to hang around and play a supporting role. There were continual interruptions from the rain, but I just plugged along.
>
> I always enjoy batting with Denise because we complement each other. We run very well together and it seems as if I'm not batting well, she is and vice versa.
>
> The other century that sticks in my mind occurred when I was playing on one and a half legs at the start of the 1989–90 season. In my first bat of the season, I got 150 not out for my club Berala. However, I missed most of that season with a knee injury which needed a couple of operations.

Lindsay, whose dad, Ian, won a rugby blue at Oxford University, was born and brought up in Zambia, came to Australia when she was 10 and probably could have played hockey for Australia if she hadn't opted for cricket.

At first, cricket was just one of the games she played with the other pupils at Ravenswood School for Girls in Sydney, along with hockey and softball. With no particular enthusiasm, Lindsay began playing schoolgirl cricket at North Sydney on Saturday afternoons, batting number 11 and making ducks.

Still, the cricketing virus got into her bloodstream and she began to hit balls against a wall for hour after hour. Reeler also practised her shots in front of a mirror, incorporating techniques from men players she admired, particularly Kim Hughes.

Like Hughes, Lindsay often threw away her wicket with a rush of blood, so she took to studying mental skills by reading books like *The Inner Game of Tennis.* She defined her goals and worked out how to achieve them.

Soon Reeler was accumulating runs by the dozen, mostly with elegant strokes after waiting for the bad ball to hit. When she dispatched the ball, it was done with a cool authority. Her cover drive is a classic.

Buoyed by words of encouragement from Allan Border and blonde hair hidden by a sunhat, Lindsay showed the killer touch in scoring 59 not out as Australia easily surpassed the English target of 127 in the 1988 World Cup final at the MCG.

'My role was to be there at the end,' she said. 'I played okay, but not as well as I can.' Nevertheless, Reeler finished the World Cup with a stupendous average of 149.33, a feat which would have made the front pages if achieved by Bradman, Chappell or Border.

Women cricketers are used to living in the shadow of their admired male counterparts. But with players like Lindsay Reeler and Denise Annetts piling up the runs in Test matches, perhaps things will change.

AUSTRALIA v ENGLAND
Collingham, 21–24 August 1987

England

	First innings		Second innings	
J. Brittin	c Matthews b Brown	56	not out	70
S. Potter	c Reeler b Larsen	16	b Fullston	8
C. Hodges	c Fullston b Owens	24	c Annetts b Owens	0
W. Watson	not out	69	c Brown b Owens	13
J. Court	b Griffiths	8	c Reeler b Goss	16
J. Powell	c Reeler b Owens	0	not out	9
J. Aspinall	c Annetts b Goss	11		
K. Hicken	c Matthews b Owens	2		
J. Chamberlain	c Fullston b Owens	2		
E. Wulcko	c Annetts b Brown	4		
G. McConway	b Owens	1		
Sundries		8		
		201		4 for 116

	O	M	R	W	O	M	R	W
Griffiths	12	2	32	1	18	7	38	0
Brown	17	7	30	2	9	4	14	0
Larsen	13	4	19	1				
Goss	18	5	32	1	11	10	1	1
Fullston	9	3	26	0	11	3	27	1
Owens	20.2	3	55	5	14	4	36	2

Fall of wickets
First innings: 34, 94, 100, 131, 138, 172, 191, 193, 200, 201
Second innings: 44, 44, 70, 87

Australia

L. Reeler	not out	110
D. Emerson	b Chamberlain	1
B. Haggett	c Hicken b Chamberlain	21
D. Annetts	run out	193
Sundries		21
		3 (dec) for 346

	O	M	R	W
Chamberlain	28	10	74	2
Aspinall	20	10	25	0
McConway	26.4	7	55	0
Potter	14	4	29	0
Hicken	25	6	48	0
Wulcko	15	1	62	0
Brittin	8	3	10	0
Hodges	5	0	23	0

Fall of wickets
First innings: 2, 37, 346

Match drawn

GRAEME HICK

Wearing Queensland's colours, Graeme Hick, the young man from Zimbabwe seen as the saviour of English cricket, plays a cut shot.

GRAEME HICK

Aficionados hailed Graeme Hick as the saviour of English cricket in 1988 when he carved an outrageous and sublime 405 not out for Worcester in a county game against Somerset at Taunton, the highest score made in England this century. After all, in three years' time this tall, disarmingly modest young man from Zimbabwe would have completed a seven-year residential qualification and be eligible to pull on an England cap.

With a combination of grace and aggression, Hick continued to pepper the pickets with some glorious stroke-play. In 1990 at the age of 24 he bettered Sir Donald Bradman's record by scoring his 50th first class century, a feat achieved by the Don when he was 26. Fittingly, Hick reached this historic mark by smashing the fastest first class century of the English season off just 71 balls to take his total to a stupendous 592 runs without being dismissed.

Graeme Ashley Hick was born in Salisbury (now Harare), Rhodesia (now Zimbabwe) on 23 May 1966, the day Joan Collins was celebrating her 33rd birthday. He was named after the great South African batsman Graeme Pollock, and from the start he was a prodigy.

Growing up on a 6,475 hectare (16,000 acre) tobacco farm managed by his father John, Hick was presented with a bat after scoring his first century for Banket Primary School against Mangula Junior School at the age of six years and eight months. His 105 not out included 24 fours, the ball racing over a hard bush ground almost devoid of grass.

Young Graeme hung a ball from an acacia tree and thumped it straight and true for hour after hour with his new bat. This might account for the way Hick is now so powerfully, innately sure through the gap between cursing bowler and hapless mid-off and mid-on.

One of these fortunate individuals who excel at all ball sports, at first Hick didn't give particular attention to cricket. He represented Zimbabwe Schools at hockey and dominated at tennis, golf and squash, with future British Open runner-up Nick Price a schoolmate at prestigious Prince Edward High School.

Just 17 and still at school, Hick played for Zimbabwe in the World Cup in England. A year later, on a Zimbabwe Cricket Union scholarship, he made his county debut in Worcestershire's final game against Surrey, batting at number nine and scoring an undefeated 82. At 20 he became the youngest player to hit up 2000 runs in an English season.

Reluctantly but understandably, Hick decided to sever the link with his native land in order to prove himself in Test cricket. New Zealand offered him a four-year qualifying period, but Hick chose a seven-year wait with England.

No matter how many Test centuries flow from his bat, Hick (who always puts his left pad on first) will forever be identified with the 405 not out at Taunton which included 11 sixes and 35 fours. He came only 19 runs short of the highest score ever made in English cricket by Archie Maclaren on the same ground way back in 1895. Without a touch of arrogance, Hick recalls:

> We were sitting at 80 for 1 when I went in and suddenly we were 130 for 5. Steve Rhodes and I batted out the rest of the day and I ended up with 179 not out. I really enjoyed getting those runs because we'd lost all those wickets.
>
> That night I asked our skipper Phil Neale what he had in mind for the next day and he said if possible he'd like to bat until tea. Then he asked if I'd set myself any career goals.
>
> I replied, 'Well, seeing you asked me, if I ever get the chance, at some stage I'd like to surpass Glenn Turner's 311 [the highest score by a Worcester batsman].'
>
> Unbelievably, it happened the very next day. Things went my way and I just kept going. I hit a couple of sixes off Brian Rose that went over mid-off. I hit the ball and looked up and hell, they'd gone for six. That was quite pleasing. Most of the 11 sixes went straight, apart from the last two which went over mid-wicket. Just scoring runs motivates me, and days like this make up for the times you get a duck.
>
> I have no hassles about Phil closing the innings when I got so close to the record. I wasn't aware of it, anyway. We had a declaration in mind at tea and I smashed the last 100 runs in hardly any time at all because I knew this.
>
> Everything just clicked. I was in that frame of mind when you sit down afterwards and say, well, it just happened. Other times you might go and bat for twice the length of time, yet you come in and can remember almost every shot.

Asked by *Wisden's Cricketers Almanack* to describe what it was like trying to stop the flow of Hick's runs, Somerset's suffering skipper Peter Roebuck declared:

> Once or twice his leg shots were lifted, but they were hit with a power that was efficient rather than savage and they thundered through or over the field. Standing erect and immense yet never imperious, Hick boomed drives to

> mid-off or through extra cover — 'not a man move' shots — and he late-cut delicately.
>
> Throughout Hick ran fast between the wickets, throughout he used a bat so broad that bowlers felt they were trying to knock down a tank with a pea-shooter. At the crease Hick avoided flamboyance and eschewed the macho. Discipline was at the core of his game. If he was bowled a good ball, he blocked it. Bad balls were hit.

That innings placed Hick among the elite band of players who completed a thousand first class runs before the end of May, and in a blazing summer he hit ten centuries, including two other doubles. The orthodoxy and straightness of his style, a strength developed by weight-lifting and a coolness which led an English commentator to describe him as the 'Bjorn Borg of cricket', ensured that this was just the start.

Of course, Hick has played many other memorable innings, and he has a special spot in his heart for his 209 against Lancashire a couple of weeks before he carved his unbeaten 405 against Somerset. He says: 'On a wicket that turned a lot, they had Jack Simmons and a left-arm spinner bowling most of the day. It was one of the most technically correct innings I've played. The next highest score in the game was 40-odd, so I really enjoyed it. I kept the good balls out and the few bad balls I got I managed to get away.'

Another magnificent innings by Hick occurred in 1989 when he virtually clinched the county championship for Worcester by leading a run chase for victory over Somerset on a dodgy wicket. With his team needing 300 runs in 57 overs, he hit up an unbeaten 136 off 168 balls under the fiercest of pressure to get Worcester home with five balls remaining.

> I enjoy my innings when we've been set a chase. When I played for Northern Districts in New Zealand, I got a double 100 against Auckland chasing 360-odd, and we won it with an over and a bit to spare. I gave a couple of chances, but chasing that sort of total I had to have a bit of luck.
>
> I find a chase in a four-day game is totally different to a one-day chase. The one-day game seems to have an air of rush about it. In a three- or four-day match you still tend to make the game safe first, but in the back of your mind you're still slightly aggressive. You're looking for the bad ball.

It was his jousts with Curtly Ambrose and Co. when the West Indies came to England the following season, rather than money, that induced Hick to have a stint with Queensland in 1990–91. With his maroon Queensland helmet, pads and bat scooped under his arm after a practice session at the Sydney Cricket Ground nets, he told me matter-of-factly:

> I know I'll get my fair share of bouncers if I get picked for England. If you bat higher up, you're going to cop it. I'll just try and stick it out and see what happens.
>
> The bouncing ball is the main reason I've come here. I wanted that experience because even on the slower wickets in England, I think the pace of the West Indies bowlers would be similar to what I've been facing in Australia.
>
> I've played against all the West Indian bowlers in county cricket, and I got 170-odd for Worcester against them at the start of their 1988 tour, too. But they will be a lot more dangerous in a Test than when they're playing in a first class match.

In Queensland, the hiring of overseas players has long been a sensitive issue as officials have been let down badly over the years by several of their recruits, and in some quarters there is strong opposition on principle to importing players on contract.

To the delight of all concerned, Hick turned out to be a dedicated, unpretentious professional who shrugged off a poor start on quicker pitches with steeper bounce to power 110 against Tasmania, 112 not out in a run chase against Western Australia and 155 against NSW. However, his footwork at times was almost non-existent.

His Queensland colleagues describe his character by pointing to the way he simply found his way to a local chemist and bought a tube of ointment when he suffered a painful heat rash in Townsville shortly after his arrival. Confronted by such circumstances, it was suggested that Queensland's previous overseas recruit, Ian Botham, would have been more likely to call in an air ambulance, a dozen nurses and a case of Bollinger.

When Ireland toured Zimbabwe several years ago, they complained that they were not meeting good enough cricketers, so Hick was called in from his coaching duties around the schools. In a one-day game against Ireland he hit 155 not out with nine sixes. The next day, a three-day match got under way against them and Hick was 112 not out overnight. The following day he went on to 309, with the next highest score being 58.

Still, the hapless Irish toilers can be cheered by the thought that they are sure to be joined in defeat by Test bowlers in all parts of the world now nice guy Graeme Hick has the chance to strut his stuff on the international stage.

WORCESTER v SOMERSET
Taunton, 5–9 May 1988

Worcester

T.S. Curtis b Rose....................................27
G.J. Lord c Mallender b Dredge 49
G.A. Hick not out..................................405
D.B. d'Oliveira c Roebuck b Rose............0
P.A. Neale c Marks b Mallender 0
I.T. Botham b Rose 7
S.J. Rhodes c Felton b Dredge 56
P.J. Newport b Marks 27
R.K. Illingworth not out 31
Sundries 26
(dec) for 628

	O	M	R	W
Jones	32	4	97	0
Mallender	32	9	86	1
Marks	50	6	141	1
Rose	31	8	101	3
Dredge	34.5	8	133	2
Roebuck	10	0	48	0

Fall of wickets: 78, 112, 112, 119, 132, 397, 451

Somerset

	First innings		Second innings	
N.A. Felton	c Radford b Hick	24	c Rhodes b Newport	36
P.M. Roebuck	lbw b Radford	0	lbw b Radford	17
J.J.E. Hardy	c Rhodes b Radford	39	b Newport	0
M.D. Crowe	c Rhodes b Newport	28	c Lord b Radford	53
R.J. Harden	lbw b Hick	2	lbw b Newport	3
V.J. Marks	c Botham b Newport	42	c Hick b Newport	7
N.D. Burns	c Botham b Radford	32	c Illingworth b Hick	11
G.D. Rose	c Curtis b Newport	12	c Rhodes b Newport	30
N.A. Mallender	c Rhodes b Newport	3	lbw b Radford	1
C.H. Dredge	b Radford	16	c Curtis b Newport	17
A.N. Jones	not out	8	not out	3
Sundries		16		14
		222		192

	O	M	R	W	O	M	R	W
Dilley	12	0	40	0	14	2	40	0
Radford	23.5	1	77	4	17	6	39	3
Newport	17	4	59	4	15.3	3	50	6
Hick	8	3	18	2	11	4	15	1
Illingworth	1	0	4	0	11	4	20	0
Botham	9	3	18	0	6	2	25	0

Fall of wickets
First innings: 1, 70, 70, 75, 147, 152, 166, 173, 203, 222
Second innings: 49, 59, 62, 74, 90, 111, 154, 167, 185, 192

Worcester won by an innings and 214 runs

MARK AND STEVE WAUGH

(Left) Mark Waugh salutes a century against England in his first Test innings in Adelaide in 1991; (right) Steve Waugh, who lost his Test spot to twin brother Mark, strikes a classical pose.

MARK AND STEVE WAUGH

The breathtaking way Mark Waugh took over from twin brother Steve and hauled Australia out of trouble against England with a glorious century in his first Test innings was more gripping than any fiction.

England was ripping through the Australian batting, with Allan Border and Dean Jones out in the space of four balls. When Mark came to the crease the Aussies were reeling at 4 for 104 in the fourth Test in Adelaide.

At the end of the opening day the English bowlers were on their knees. Waugh had carved an unbeaten 116 off only 144 balls with 16 fours, five of them being carved from 10 deliveries in the first two overs of spinner Phil Tufnell. The second 50 of his ton came in just 52 balls.

No longer would Mark be known as Afghanistan, the forgotten Waugh. With a deceptively lazy swing of his 2lb 10oz bat, he produced one elegant stroke after another, clipping the ball off his pads and spearing shots through the covers.

Mark then went back to the Adelaide dressing room and drew a little stick figure on his thigh pad as he does every time he posts a first class century. 'It's something I picked up from Keith Fletcher [the former England captain] when I went to play for Essex — like a gun-fighter putting a notch on his belt.'

With more than 3000 runs flowing from Mark's bat in 1990, causing him to be named as one of Wisden's five Cricketers of the Year, justice had demanded that Waugh be given his chance in the highest company through sheer weight of performance, but naturally he would have preferred to win a Test cap at the expense of somebody other than brother Steve. An amiable fellow with a happy smile, Mark recalls how he dug Australia out of a hole with his maiden Test century:

> I was round at Mum and Dad's place when Steve came round and broke the news. 'Congratulations,' he said. 'You're in.' Finally I asked, 'Who's out?' Steve replied, 'Me, but I'm just another player.' We sat there stunned for about three minutes with nobody saying a word. Obviously I'd rather have taken someone else's place, but I always thought my turn would come in a Test if I kept scoring runs.
>
> Of all the wickets in the world to make your debut on, you'd have to pick Adelaide. I'd played two previous first class innings there and got 70-odd and

172. I roomed with Merv Hughes, and if I had any tension, he relieved it and I had a good night's sleep before the Test. Merv is a great fun sort of fellow.

Nobody had time to wish me luck when I went out to bat because everything happened in such a rush. Everyone sits up front in Adelaide, with the changing room being down below. One moment I'm putting my pads on, then Jonesy got out and I was on my way to the crease.

I'll always remember my first scoring shot — a three straight down the ground. Second ball from Phillip De Freitas. I wasn't nervous to start with. It was one of those days when everything hit the middle of the bat, one of those one-in-a-hundred digs.

Once I got a few runs, I forgot what sort of game I was playing in. I just wanted to stabilise the innings, and was concentrating so hard I forgot about everything else around me. If there was any niggling, I didn't hear it. I just tried to play my shots. Play naturally.

When Greg Matthews came in, we needed a big partnership and he held up an end while I played my shots. We'd batted together quite a bit for NSW, and our left-hand/right-hand combination helps break up the bowler's line and length. After each over we said a few things. Nothing special. Keep going, keep concentrating. That sort of stuff.

The other stroke I remember was the one that gave me my 100. I was 97 and hit Tufnell through the covers for four. Graham Gooch, my captain at Essex, was over like a shot. 'Well done, boy,' he said. I felt that deep down he had wanted me to do well, even though he was desperate for a win over Australia.

It was the best innings technically I've ever played. I think I play a bit better under pressure, and it might have been a bit harder for me had I been leaving the dressing room at 4 for 400 instead of 4 for 100-odd. I woke up a few times that night wondering whether I'd get to 150 or even 200, but I needn't have bothered as I played on to Devon Malcolm when I'd made 138. Still, you can't do much better than a 100 in your first Test innings. I got a telegram from Stephen saying congratulations.

Richie Benaud was moved to comment: 'I find it difficult to recall a better innings on debut in Test cricket, and the thing I liked most was that Waugh played very much in an Australian way. He carried the attack to England, tore away from them the advantage they so deservedly held.'

Mark's debut century was in sharp contrast to brother Steve's long and puzzling wait for a Test 100 which finally came against England at Leeds in 1989, in his 42nd innings in his 27th Test.

Upon reaching 99, Steve tried to chew a wad of gum but there was no saliva in his mouth. Then he clipped a ball from Phil Newport deep to point for a single, joyfully leapt in the air and frantically waved his bat in the direction of the Australian dressing room to celebrate as good a 100 as he will ever hit.

After the frustrations of being the victim of some diabolical umpiring decisions in Pakistan and then being dismissed for 90 and 91 against the West Indies, there was no way Waugh was going to bottle up his emotions. The gorilla was off his back. The burden had been lifted, the critics silenced.

His chanceless century was posted off just 124 balls and the man they call Tugga carried on with some devastating stroke-play to finish with 177 not out. It was one of the greatest Test knocks in years, full of square drives and cuts which speared off his bat — a stylish Monet fashioned with a piece of willow rather than a paint brush and oils.

Then it was on to Lord's for the second Test in which Steve, with elegance to match the setting, hit up 152 not out, prompting the British Sunday papers to go right over the top. The *Sunday Express* declared, 'David Gower and his players have been utterly demoralised by the brilliance of Steve Waugh, who may walk like Charlie Chaplin but is looking more like Don Bradman every day.' The *Mail on Sunday* commented, 'If his 177 not out at Leeds was a case of cashing in on cafeteria bowling, this was sheer haute cuisine.'

When Waugh boosted his run splurge with 21 not out in the second innings at Lord's, he indeed had the Bradman-like tally of 350 runs without being dismissed. Riding his luck in the third Test at Edgbaston, he blazed his way to 43 off only 54 balls before Angus Fraser knocked back his stumps to leave Steve with the staggering Test average of 393. It was the most runs ever scored in any Test series without the player being dismissed.

Waugh followed up with 92 at Old Trafford, a duck at Trent Bridge ('You're only as good as your last innings,' was Dean Jones' greeting when he got back to the dressing room) and 14 and 7 not out at The Oval to finish the series with 506 runs at a stupendous average of 126.50 per innings.

Quiet, lean and self effacing with a quick smile, Steve Waugh recalls his 177 not out at Leeds thus:

> It was just one of those days when I made up my mind to go out and play some shots. The century was long overdue and while it was a bit of weight on my shoulders, I was never too worried about getting it. I've always said I'd rather be consistent than score 100 followed by three or four low scores.
>
> I played and missed a couple before a front foot push to the off went for

four. That got the confidence going. Running with Dean Jones helped, too. We'd pick up quick singles and turn twos into threes. You always get nervous in the 90s, so there was no real difference this time. When I reached 90 against the West Indies in Brisbane the previous season I got out to the hardest shot I hit in the game. Straight to Desmond Haynes at extra cover. This time I got the century off my first ball on 99 and just went on and on.

The wickets in England tend to suit me because they are a bit slower and I can play my cut shots and force harder off the back foot. However, I hadn't made a Test century in 26 matches and badly needed the confidence which a big century brings. Once I did it there was no reason at all why I couldn't go out and do it again. Now I have that feeling every time I bat. The breakthrough of that 177 at Leeds changed my level of expectation.

I was a lot more relaxed when I proved I could do it again by making a century in the next Test at Lord's. It was a lot easier this time and I raced to 80 or 90. But of the two, I would say the 177 was the better innings. That day I played as well as I have ever played.

It's funny really, you go for so long without a Test 100, but if you continue to put in all the hard work, it suddenly comes. Bobby Simpson told me he had to wait ages for his first Test 100 and look what he achieved. There is enough pressure in Test cricket, so although I wanted a century, I was prepared to be reasonably patient. I just hoped the selectors would be, too.

Surprisingly, Waugh overlooks these magnificent centuries against England in choosing his most memorable century. Instead he goes for an innings of 111 not out for Somerset against Surrey at The Oval in an English county match in 1987. With Sylvester Clarke taking the new ball for Surrey, it was Steve's first ever taste of West Indian firepower. Waugh recalls:

It was my third game for Somerset, so I was out to prove myself. We were in a lot of trouble at 6 for 110-odd, so it was going to be a good test of skill against a guy who was going to be much quicker than anything I'd ever faced. Clarke just ambled up to the wicket and let it rip. All shoulders. The ball was a blur as it whipped past, even sharper than I'd expected. Jeez, I'll really have to be on my toes. Against a guy of this pace, it's a matter of survival more than anything. If I don't concentrate 100 per cent, I could be injured or get out. In the end I finished up with 111 not out — nothing spectacular but one of the most important innings of my life and my first century in county cricket. By adjusting to a pace and bounce I hadn't struck before, I proved to myself that I wasn't going to be blown away when Australia played the West Indies later in the year. Knowing I could do it, it was a totally different experience facing a

> guy of Clarke's quickness who was swinging it and doing a bit with the ball, and to bat against that sort of pace really sharpened me up. The West Indian guys play the game hard but they don't talk a lot. Just a few nasty stares. When you're bowling that quick, there's no need to say that much.

Stephen Rodger Waugh and his twin Mark were born in Sydney on 2 June 1965, Steve being the elder by four minutes. Their eyes and reflexes sharpened by dad Rodger throwing them tennis balls in the backyard of their Panania home, Steve and Mark represented NSW in soccer, cricket and tennis at primary school level, their matching Prince Valiant haircuts making them instantly recognisable. Asked what they wanted to do with their lives, they'd say, 'Play cricket for Australia.'

In 1988, the Waughs became the first twins to play cricket for Australia when chosen in a one day match against the West Indies; Mark ended up running out his brother. Mark was playing for Essex when Steve toured England with the Australian team a year later; each twin scored 100 not out in a game at Chelmsford.

In batting ability there was little to choose between the Waugh brothers, with free spirit Mark the more extravagant and Steve the more quietly competitive. It was Steve who won an Esso Scholarship to play for Essex Second XI, where he hit a century for Ilford against Chingford off 28 balls. Their mother Bev, who won a State Under-14 tennis title, says: 'I've always stressed that they should not lose their cool, that they should analyse what they've done wrong and done right, give credit where it's due and fight back.'

'Waughsome', thundered the headlines when Steve and Mark hit up blazing double centuries (216 not out and 229 not out respectively) to post a world record fifth wicket partnership of 464 for NSW against Western Australia in Perth in 1990. Their unbroken stand was also an Australian record for any wicket. Mark plundered a WA attack headed by Test pair Terry Alderman and Bruce Reid for 35 fours and a six while Steve struck a mere 21 fours. Mark says:

> After my debut Test century, this was my next best innings. I'd never got runs in Perth before, maybe because it's such a different wicket after playing so much in Sydney. They had a good attack, too. Bruce Reid, Terry Alderman, Chris Matthews and Ken MacLeay.
>
> NSW were in trouble and it doesn't happen too often that Stephen and I get a lot of runs together. We just played our own game and never tried to out-do each other. As I'd done after my two other double centuries, I got the thigh pad and drew a stick figure with two heads, four arms and four legs.

Steve originally was a speculative choice by the Australian selectors against India in 1985 to fill part of the gap left by the retirement of Greg Chappell, Dennis Lillee and Rod Marsh and the defection of other leading players to the lure of South African Kruger-Rands. On the evidence of his dashing stroke-play in a tight Sheffield Shield final at the Sydney Cricket Ground, it was felt Waugh had a bright future. He reminded many aficionados of Doug Walters, only with a better technique. He played the ball very late, using his wrists to whip it away with superlative timing.

In his early Tests, Steve showed up more as an all-rounder: a small contribution with the ball here, a mini innings there and brilliant fielding everywhere. This was enough to retain his place in the Australian side.

After his disastrous tour of Pakistan, Waugh fearlessly played his shots against the thunderballs of the West Indian pace bowlers in a manner which suggested he was soon to pay a handsome dividend on the original investment by the Australian selectors. Typically, when he returned to the dressing room after scoring his initial Test century against England, one of his first acts was to thank chairman of selectors Lawrie Sawle for sticking with him so long.

During Australia's 1987 World Cup triumph in India and Pakistan, Waugh made such a crucial contribution that team coach Bob Simpson called him the ice man. 'I take that as a compliment,' Waugh says. 'I did fairly well in a couple of tight situations. It's important to remain cool under pressure.'

The last few overs of a one-day international are dreaded by most bowlers, who fear they will turn out to be a feather duster rather than a plumed peacock. For this job, Waugh volunteered. In the World Cup, he bowled the final over against India and ensured that Australia won its opening game by a single run, by bowling Maninder Singh with the second last ball.

In the final over against New Zealand, Waugh removed Martin Crowe and Ian Smith with successive balls and ran out Martin Snedden. When Australia reached the semi-final at Lahore, Steve carved 18 runs from Saleem Jaffer in Australia's last over against Pakistan and plunged a huge, bubbling crowd into silence by ensuring his team had a match-winning total.

In the World Cup final at Eden Gardens, Calcutta, with England wanting 19 off two overs, two nerveless slower balls from Waugh followed by his dismissal of Phillip De Freitas snuffed out the English team's hopes.

In 1988, Waugh was named one of Wisden's five Cricketers of the Year after coming to Somerset's rescue following the loss of Viv Richards, Ian Botham and Joel Garner and then Martin Crowe. His superlative summer produced more than 2000 runs, with 1314 (including six centuries) in 15 first class matches at an average of 73. Typically, Waugh didn't have a clue he had reached the remarkable milestone of 1000 runs in June until the scorer told him he had broken the barrier with his fifth century of the month for Somerset on the last day of June. In his lively book, *Diary of the Ashes*, Test and NSW colleague Geoff Lawson says:

> For someone so compact and ordered on the field, Tugga is amazingly untidy off it. He's forever losing things, wallet or keys in his hotel room, batting gloves, socks and shirts in the dressing room. His kit is so messy that when he's packing it after a game, he has to stand on it while someone clips it shut. One day he even left his suitcase in a hotel room.
>
> Waughie is quiet and self-effacing off the field, but once he walks through the gate, look out. He's one of the most competitive people I've met. It doesn't matter who's at the other end batting or bowling, he'll back his ability against theirs.

In Brisbane in the first Test against the West Indies in 1988, Waugh rocked colleagues by whipping down three bouncers at Viv Richards, while in the 1989 tour opener at Worcester, he tried out Ian Botham with a couple of bumpers.

With brother Mark's run glut demanding that he be given a chance in the Tests against England, Steve was the one to go because he had been struggling to find his proper form. Three months later, on 9 April 1991 at Port-of-Spain, Trinidad, Steve walked out to join Mark at the crease in the third Test against the West Indies, making them the first twins to bat together in 114 years of Test cricket. Asked why the brothers hadn't acknowledged each other either at the start or finish of their 58-run partnership, Mark explained: 'That's how it always is. Yeah, it was a special moment, but once you're out there you've got a job to do for your country.' Simple as that.

AUSTRALIA v ENGLAND
Adelaide, 25–29 January 1991

Australia

G. Marsh c Gooch b Small	37	c Gooch b Small 0
M. Taylor run out	5	run out 4
D. Boon c Fraser b Malcolm	49	b Tufnell 121
A. Border b De Freitas	12	(7) not out 83
D. Jones lbw b De Freitas	0	(4) lbw b De Freitas 8
M. Waugh b Malcolm	138	(5) b Malcolm 23
G. Matthews c Stewart b Gooch	65	(8) not out 34
I. Healy c Stewart b De Freitas	1	
C. McDermott not out	42	
M. Hughes lbw b Small	1	(6) c Gooch b Fraser 30
B. Reid c Lamb b De Freitas	5	
Sundries	31	11
	386	6 (dec) for 314

	O	M	R	W	O	M	R	W
Malcolm	38	7	104	2	21	0	87	1
Fraser	23	6	48	0	26	3	66	1
Small	34	10	92	2	18	3	64	1
De Freitas	26.2	6	56	4	23	6	61	1
Tufnell	5	0	38	0	16	3	28	1
Gooch	9	2	23	1				

Fall of wickets
First innings: 11, 62, 104, 104, 124, 295, 298, 358, 373, 386
Second innings: 1, 8, 25, 64, 130, 240

England

G. Gooch c Healy b Reid	87	c Marsh B Reid 117
M. Atherton lbw b McDermott	0	c Waugh b Reid
A. Lamb c Healy b McDermott	0	b McDermott 53
R. Smith c and b Hughes	53	(5) not out 10
D. Gower c Hughes b McDermott	11	(4) lbw b Hughes 16
A. Stewart c Healy b Reid	11	c Jones b McDermott 9
P. De Freitas c Matthews b McDermott	45	not out 19
G. Small b McDermott	1	
A. Fraser c Healy b Reid	2	
D. Malcolm c Healy b Reid	2	
P. Tufnell not out	0	
Sundries	17	24
	229	5 for 335

	O	M	R	W	O	M	R	W
Reid	29	9	53	4	23	5	59	2
McDermott	26.3	3	97	5	27	5	106	2
Hughes	22	4	62	1	14	3	52	1
Waugh	4	1	13	0	1	0	4	0
Matthews					31	7	100	0

Fall of wickets
First innings: 10, 11, 137, 160, 176, 179, 198, 215, 219, 229
Second innings: 203, 246, 287, 287, 297

SOMERSET v SURREY
The Oval, 19–21 August 1987

Somerset

N.A. Felton c Stewart b Clarke	4	c Jesty b Greig	22
P.M. Roebuck b Greig	54	lbw b Clarke	59
J.J.E. Hardy c Stewart b Bicknell	59	c Doughty b Clarke	16
R.J. Harden c Stewart b Greig	0	c Stewart b Clarke	0
S.R. Waugh b Bicknell	8	not out	111
N.J. Pringle c Stewart b Bicknell	30	c Stewart b Clarke	0
N.D. Burns c Lynch b Clarke	9	c sub b Clarke	0
V.J. Marks not out	27	b Medlycott	35
G.D. Rose c Stewart b Bicknell	6	c Jesty b Greig	7
G.V. Palmer c Grieg b Bicknell	0	c Greig b Medlycott	0
A.N. Jones b Bicknell	9	c Doughty b Bicknell	15
Sundries	16		26
	222		291

	O	M	R	W	O	M	R	W
Clarke	22	6	49	2	32	11	74	5
Bicknell	24.2	6	63	6	27	7	76	1
Doughty	13	3	38	0	13	0	38	0
Greig	28	9	57	2	23	2	64	2
Medlycott	5	2	6	0	13	9	16	2

Fall of wickets
First innings: 5, 98, 100, 121, 146, 163, 192, 204, 204, 222
Second innings: 53, 99, 99, 110, 110, 114, 215, 234, 239, 291

Surrey

G.S. Clinton c Burns b Marks	66	(11) not out	0
D.M. Smith c Waugh b Rose	7	c Marks b Rose	4
A.J. Stewart st Burns b Marks	105	c Harden b Jones	93
M.A. Lynch c Roebuck b Rose	1	(1) lbw b Rose	9
D.M. Ward b Waugh	17	b Waugh	43
K.T. Medlycott b Palmer	13	(7) b Waugh	14
I.A. Greig c Pringle b Marks	15	(6) c Hardy b Waugh	7
T.E. Jesty c Rose b Palmer	21	(4) c Harden b Marks	17
R.J. Doughty c and b Palmer	0	(8) c Burns b Jones	5
S.T. Clarke not out	6	(9) c Burns b Jones	1
M.P. Bicknell b Palmer	18	(10) not out	0
Sundries	28		18
	297		9 for 211

	O	M	R	W	O	M	R	W
Jones	17	2	51	0	7	0	55	3
Rose	15	3	48	2	8	0	29	2
Waugh	18	5	63	1	11	0	48	3
Palmer	16	3	64	3	3	0	20	0
Marks	16	4	56	3	7	0	42	1

Fall of wickets
First innings: 28, 148, 156, 173, 196, 241, 273, 273, 273, 297
Second innings: 15, 20, 50, 137, 153, 205, 210, 211, 211

Match drawn

DEAN JONES

Dean Jones, the king of one-day cricket, oozes arrogance and confidence as he lofts one for six.

DEAN JONES

With white sun cream melting from his cracked lips, Dean Jones pushed himself almost to death's door in putting together a monumental 210 in Australia's tied Test with India in Madras in September 1986.

Batting for almost two days in searing heat and humidity, with temperatures reaching 42 and 43 degrees Celsius in the dusty concrete bowl of the Chepauk stadium, Jones became fever-stricken and kept vomiting beside the pitch. Twice the Victorian urinated in his pants.

Running twos and threes was out of the question, so Jones and Allan Border simply walked singles and hit boundaries. Hardly able to stand after passing 160, Jones tottered down the wicket to his skipper.

'Mate, I've had enough,' Jones gasped. 'I can't move my arms. I've just pissed in my pants again and I'm a mess.'

'Okay,' Border replied, adding wickedly, 'We'll get a really tough Australian out here. A Queenslander. We'll get Fat Cat. He'll handle the job.' Greg Ritchie was to come in next.

Stung by Border's words, Jones somehow carried on to reach his double century and it wasn't until he was bowled 20 minutes after tea while swiping at spinner Shivlal Yadav that the gravity of his journey between hell and high valour emerged.

Feeling better after sinking into a cold tub, Jones got up . . . and awakened in hospital with a saline drip in his arm. Only then was it fully realised that he had risked irreversible physical damage to boost Australia's cause. Jones had lost 15.4 lb (7 kg) in a day and was suffering from dangerous dehydration. Australian coach Bob Simpson says bluntly, 'No one has ever been asked for more on a cricket field.'

Showing a new-found patience, Jones had played second fiddle to century-maker David Boon on the first day to finish with 56 at stumps after a stay of four and half hours. Recalling that epic innings in just his third Test, Jones, who was chosen ahead of Mike Veletta only on the morning of the match, says:

> I don't really remember a hell of a lot after I hit an on-drive for four off Ravi Shastri to reach 100. It was just so bloody hot. Forty degrees and 90 per cent humidity, with the stench of sewerage from a big canal outside the ground. Their keeper had gone off after 45 minutes on the first day suffering from dehydration.

I was so tired I couldn't run twos or threes, and I was vomiting a lot. I even urinated in my pants a couple of times. I just couldn't help myself. The guys were running out with drinks every two or three overs, but I couldn't keep any liquids down. My boots were full of sweat and it was like standing in a bucket of water. The white sun cream kept melting off my lips and nose. It was just real hard yakka.

I couldn't eat at lunch, nor could I keep any liquids down. I was sucking on glucose tablets in the hope of getting some energy, but it was a waste of time. Back on the field, Sunny Gavaskar, the Indian captain, kept telling me to try a lime juice drink instead of water.

We still were under a bit of pressure because we thought the wicket was going to break up later on, so it was good to be batting with Allan Border. He'd given me so much strength before the game when he said I had the talent to bat number three for Australia for as long as I wanted. I'd been under a bit of pressure from Mike Veletta, and after that talk in AB's room I knew in my heart I was going to get runs.

By the time I'd reached 160, I'd got to the stage where I'd block two balls and try to slog the next one. I'd got pins and needles in my arms and was crampy. I couldn't sweep because every time I'd go on to one knee and try to play the shot, I'd cramp up. It was a waste of time staying there.

When I went down the pitch and told AB I'd had enough, he shot back his remark about getting a really tough Australian. A Queenslander. It was the best thing he could have said to me.

'Right,' I said, 'I'm staying in.' If he'd just said Greg Ritchie, I probably would have gone off. But when he said a Queenslander, that was it. I had to stay out there.

I reached 200 with a little squirt through first slip off one of the spinners. Then we went in for tea and I thought I was finished. But the guys stripped me off, threw me under the shower and because I didn't have the strength to put my clothes back on, they dressed me and pushed me out the door. One problem. They forgot to put on my thigh pad and box.

When I got out I went into the shower and then they put me in a bath full of ice to cool me down. I was able to keep down a couple of drinks before getting onto the rub-down table. Next thing I started cramping badly all over my body. In the stomach, thighs, head, neck, everywhere. Next thing I was rushed to hospital where I woke to find a drip in my arm.

I stayed there until two o'clock in the morning. When our physio, Errol Alcott, asked how I felt, I said, 'I want to get back with the boys.' I slept in Errol's room and after having a swim in the morning, I felt a bit better and could eat a little food.

I'd lost 7 kg in a day and it took me six months to get that weight back on.

For a while I couldn't handle the sun at all. I couldn't go out for any more than two hours at a time and it was three or four weeks before I could put together a good score again.

I suppose your first Test century always sticks in the memory and because the game provided only the second tie in the history of Test cricket, that 210 against India remains my most memorable innings.

Oozing arrogance and confidence, Jones refuses to allow bowlers to dictate to him; if necessary, he'll hit over the top. Tall and elegant as he munches gum at the crease, the Victorian can play the drive on both sides of the wicket, the pull and the hook, and when he plays forward he takes a big, decisive stride. With superb footwork, Jones can improvise brilliantly and on his best days he can be virtually impossible to bowl to.

His cricketing genes come from dad Barney, whose aggressive leadership of Carlton made him something of a legendary figure in Melbourne club cricket. Young Dean would watch his father in action and listen in rapture when Keith Stackpole and English Test star John Snow came to tea.

At first Jones was an impetuous dasher without a clue how to build an innings, causing The *Australian*'s Terry Brindle to comment: 'Dangerously cavalier when he should be effectively roundhead. Too much talent and not enough tungsten.'

After missing the 1985 tour to England, Jones fought back to win a spot on the trip to India where he broke through with his courageous 210. Dropped again after scoring a mere 44 runs at 8.80 in three Tests against Pakistan in 1988, Dean clawed his way back and when he scored his first 13 runs against the West Indies in the Boxing Day Test in Adelaide with straight drives, he knew he had recaptured his old touch. The result was an innings of 216 which ensured he was on the plane to England.

In the erratic early stages of Jones' Test career, New Zealand champion Richard Hadlee declared he didn't rate Dean as a first drop and kept knocking him over to prove it. He also expressed grave doubts over the Victorian's ability to succeed in England.

Relishing a drop to number five in the Ashes Tests in England in 1989, Jones scored 566 runs at 70.75, including 157 at Edgbaston and 122 at The Oval. Despite suffering a triple fracture of the cheekbone while attempting to hook against Sussex early in the tour, Jones piled up 1510 runs at 88.82 to head the first class figures on the trip.

When Jones came back to the crease after having his cheekbone fractured at Hove, Steve Waugh, who was on 71, walked up and said, 'You shouldn't be here, Deano. I don't care about making a century.' Jones replied, 'Don't worry about me. I'll beat you to 100.' He hit the next ball from Tony Dodemaide for six!

Jones was ordered to wear a grill-mask to avoid permanent damage to his optic nerve following the Sussex mishap; however, he decided to discard the grill after scoring a less than totally satisfying 146 runs in his first four Test innings, including a last-up duck at Lord's. With guru Geoff Boycott advising him not to worry, simply play a bit straighter, he promptly hit up 157 spread over three days in a rain-affected third Test.

Australian coach Bob Simpson recalls: 'The big thing about Deano is that he works the ball so well and is such a good runner that he's extremely difficult to contain. When we had lost some early wickets against England, he marched in and smashed 14 off John Emburey's next two overs and the pressure was suddenly off. Jones had a difficult patch with Hadlee, but his career was resurrected because we had faith in him and he's repaid that.'

Jones returned home to carve an unfinished record sixth-wicket partnership of 260 with Steve Waugh against the hapless Sri Lankans in Hobart, contributing 118 not out to lift his calendar year's Test aggregate to a stunning 1099 runs at the remarkable average of 73.27.

The best runners between wickets in the game, and equally capable of ripping any attack to shreds, Jones and Waugh are unchallenged as the most dangerous middle-order pair in world cricket. Jones explains:

> Because of his pace, Steve is the best runner I've run with between wickets. We like running hard and when he comes in we always say, 'Right, we'll run them off their legs.' We love pressurising the guys. I probably get more fun out of pinching a two than I do hitting a four. By putting pressure on the fieldsmen, all of a sudden you get them worrying and they're liable to do something silly. They really hate it.
>
> It's not so much pace that gives quickness running between wickets. David Boon is not the fastest guy over 22 yards, but he's very quick in and out of the box as we call it. It's all in the turn. I concentrate on running straight at the point where I want to turn and come straight out without circling at the crease. Because this technique has become vitally important in cricket, I've really worked hard to get it right.
>
> It's good fun batting with Steve Waugh because there's always something happening. We like to get stuck into them, no matter who they are. We get confidence from each other. We somehow decide to nail them and that's that. I don't like playing dull matches or dull cricket. I want to play good exciting cricket.

With scalps of 210 against India, 216 off the West Indies, 184 not out against England in Sydney in 1986–87 and a stupendous 102 not out off only 91 balls against New Zealand in a one-day final in Auckland in 1990 hanging from his belt, Jones has some golden memories. How does he rate these centuries?

> I only rate 100s in winning teams. The double century against the West Indies helped me get picked for the English tour, but I put the 184 not out against England ahead of it because it was in a winning team after we'd been 2–0 down. It's very important to get runs in the first innings in Sydney as it's a lot harder to get them in the second innings because of the wicket. That 184 gave me 500 runs in a losing series, and I was quite happy about that.
>
> I rate the 102 not out in New Zealand because it was in a final. You make 100s in one-day finals, then you win. I enjoyed that 145 [four sixes and 12 fours] I got against England in a one-dayer in Brisbane in 1990. I got 120-odd against Pakistan at the WACA, but we lost that game so it never really counted. I'd rather take the 70s when we win. I scored a 90 in Sydney against the West Indies, but it was a waste of time making them because we lost.

In light of his horror tour to Pakistan in 1988, to which the finale was a pair of ducks in the third Test in Lahore, Jones took much delight in carving 116 and 121 not out against Imran Khan's Pakistanis in the second Test in Adelaide in January 1990. At no stage in his five-and-a-half hour first innings vigil could he relax and indulge himself in the riveting clash with Pakistan's superb fast bowler Wasim Akram. It was white-knuckle stuff, as Jones explains:

> Guys like Wasim know how to swing the old ball and they always make you work hard. Some Test bowlers give you the odd freebie, but I don't remember too many balls I could just leave alone. They know how to bowl on flat wickets, and Akram is always looking to wear you down. I hadn't been playing straight enough, but I worked hard on it with help from Bob Simpson and it came right.

Although hit an excruciating blow on the elbow, Jones pluckily hit up an unbeaten 121 in the second innings to give Australia a draw, thus becoming only the tenth Australian to score a century in each innings of a Test.

His play in this Test was an eye-opener to those who pigeon-holed Jones as a blithe spirit in the middle order rather than a man capable of playing long, defensive innings to get his team out of trouble. He proved he could both absorb and plunder, the mark of an exceptional player.

No wonder Yorkshire was so keen for Jones to make history by becoming the famous county's first overseas professional. With Geoff Boycott leading the push, it seemed a fait accompli until Brian Close, the former England and Yorkshire skipper, stepped in and overthrew the vote.

Boycott is internationally respected as one of cricket's deepest thinkers, so Jones sought his advice when he was a young man playing league cricket in England; he is not afraid to seek a refresher course, either. He contacted the Yorkshireman after his horror trip to Pakistan and again during the 1989 tour of England. Jones explains, 'Boycott is a straight shooter and gives you frank opinions and I respond to that because I always get the same attitude from Keith Stackpole and Bob Simpson. If you really want to know where you stand, they give you both barrels.'

In 1989–90 there was an outcry when Imran Khan and not Jones was announced as winner of the $72,000 International Cricketer of the Year award, even though the Australian had hit three Test centuries, plus 99 against New Zealand, and was the outstanding player of the World Series Cup. Although his favourite bat had been stolen in Sydney that week, Jones promptly smashed an unbeaten 83 from Imran, Wasim Akram and Co. to sink Pakistan in Melbourne in the first Cup final play-off.

Then it was off to New Zealand where Jones hoisted Australia to victory in the one-day Cup final against New Zealand with a stunning 102 not out with five sixes, two of them off Richard Hadlee. With his brilliant fielding and dashing batting, he was unchallenged as the world's best in the slap and dash of one-day cricket. However, Jones is adamant Pakistan's Javed Miandad is the top one-day player and explains:

> I've picked up a lot of my one-day cricket from Javed. I just love the cheeky way he bats. He can hit, he can bunt and create singles. He's aggressive and turns ones into twos. He annoys fielders and he annoys bowlers, and that's something I try to do. No one will ever match the power of Viv Richards, but Javed's ability to work the ball and keep things moving gives him the edge as a one-day player.

At the crease Jones is a constant chatterer because he has so much nervous energy. He can annoy bowlers by saying such things as 'You can't bowl there to me and get away with it', or 'No need to run for that one.' He says:

> I talk to myself to get geed up and my batting partner, too, and I might mention a couple of things to bowlers if I think I've got them or I'm trying to put them off their game a bit. You should never sledge a fast bowler, though,

because it's only going to help him. But I'll have a little word to a spin bowler here and there. In the mind game, it can help if you've got a guy worried about what I'm doing instead of what he's doing.

Summing up his strengths, Jones says:

I think slow wickets suit me — India, England, New Zealand. I tend to struggle at certain times against really good quicks on bouncy wickets, but so does everyone, I suppose.

Provided I'm a bit short of the ball, I might try to get up and under it, but I think my strength is hitting the ball wide of mid-off and mid-on and using my strength and using my feet. Which is good in a way because it breaks up a bowler's length. I might be batting with Geoff Marsh or David Boon, who are very good cutters and sweepers who tend to stay at the crease. We complement each other and it stuffs up the bowler's line and length.

The big thing about this Australian team is that we help each other. If my batting partner picks something I'm doing wrong, he tells me and I'll take the advice. We're winning, so we can carry players who are struggling a bit. The guys carried me when we were losing a bit, and now hopefully I can pay them back.

AUSTRALIA v INDIA
Madras, 18–22 September 1986

Australia

	First innings		Second innings	
D.C. Boon	c Kapil Dev b Sharma	122	lbw b Maninder	49
G.R. Marsh	c Kapil Dev b Yadav	22	b Shastri	11
D.M. Jones	b Yadav	210	c Azharuddin b Maninder	24
R.J. Bright	c Shastri b Yadav	30		
A.R. Border	c Gavaskar b Shastri	106	b Maninder	27
G.M. Ritchie	run out	13	c Pandit b Shastri	28
G.R.J. Matthews	c Pandit b Yadav	44	not out	27
S.R. Waugh		12	not out	2
Sundries		15		2
		7 (dec) for 574		5 (dec) for 170

	O	M	R	W	O	M	R	W
Kapil Dev	18	5	52	0	1	0	5	0
Chetan Sharma	16	1	70	1	6	0	19	0
Maninder	39	8	135	0	19	2	60	0
Yadav	49.5	9	142	4	9	0	35	0
Shastri	47	8	161	1	14	2	50	2
Srikkanth	1	0	6	0				

Fall of wickets
First innings: 48, 206, 282, 460, 481, 544, 574
Second innings: 31, 81, 94, 125, 165

India

	First innings		Second innings	
S.M. Gavaskar	c and b Matthews	8	c Jones b Bright	90
K. Srikkanth	c Ritchie b Matthews	53	c Waugh b Matthews	39
M.B. Amarnath	run out	1	c Boon b Matthews	51
M. Azharuddin	c and b Bright	50	c Ritchie b Bright	42
R.J. Shastri	c Zoehrer b Matthews	62	(7) not out	48
C.S. Pandit	c Waugh b Matthews	35	(5) b Matthews	39
Kapil Dev	c Border b Matthews	119	(6) c Bright b Matthews	1
K.S. More	c Zoehrer b Waugh	4	(9) lbw b Bright	0
Chetan Sharma	c Zoehrer b Reid	30	(8) c McDermott b Bright	23
N.S. Yadav	c Border b Bright	19	b Bright	8
Maninder Singh	not out	0	lbw b Matthews	0
Sundries		16		6
		397		347

	O	M	R	W	O	M	R	W
McDermott	14	2	59	0	5	0	27	0
Reid	18	4	93	1	10	2	48	0
Matthews	28.2	3	103	5	39.5	7	146	5
Bright	23	3	88	2	25	3	94	5
Waugh	11	2	44	1	4	1	16	0
Border								

Fall of wickets
First innings: 62, 65, 65, 142, 206, 220, 245, 330, 387, 397
Second innings: 55, 158, 204, 251, 253, 291, 331, 334, 334, 347

Match tied

MARK TAYLOR

Mark Taylor, the man who set Australia's innings in concrete, smacks one through the covers for four.

MARK TAYLOR

Discussing his world record Test score of 365, Sir Gary Sobers paid the ultimate compliment to Mark Taylor when he said:

> I have always said records are there to be broken, but this one presents special problems. The player who beats it will have to bat fairly quickly, otherwise it will ruin his side's chance of winning the match. I don't see a number four or five batsman breaking the record. There is not enough time. An opening bat gets a far better chance.
>
> I have my doubts about Graeme Hick. There is a big difference between county and Test cricket. I fancy Mark Taylor, the Australian opener, more because he has tremendous concentration, great ability and can score at the required pace.

After a nerve-racking opening to his Test career in 1989 against Viv Richards' West Indians, left-hander Taylor went to England and won instant fame as the man who sets Australia's innings in concrete. In six Tests, he played quite superbly to accumulate 839 runs at the Bradman-like average of 83.9, including an elegantly crafted score of 219. His handsome cover-drive was straight out of the coaching manual as he dwarfed the 1948 English tour deeds of Australia's famed left-handed opener, Arthur Morris. Only Sir Donald Bradman and England's Wally Hammond have scored more runs in a Test series.

The man they call Tub was an automatic choice as one of Wisden's five Cricketers of the Year. Taylor returned home to peel off another four Test centuries against Sri Lanka and Pakistan. Thwarting Pakistan's extremely talented pace attack headed by Wasim Akram, with two centuries in three Tests, Taylor's triumphs prompted losing skipper Imran Khan to claim the Australian opener was the difference between the two teams.

Well aware that yesterday's hero wraps up tomorrow's fish and chips, Taylor summed up his purple patch:

> Really, it was ridiculous, jumping straight from obscurity to being compared with Bradman. It had its pluses, though. I may turn out to be one of the biggest flops of all time, but at least I'll be able to tell my grandchildren that for one series I was compared with Sir Donald Bradman.
>
> I don't think you can put it down to luck because I like to think I'm a good player, but I did go through a hot streak. I know I'm going to have some bad

times, so I try to be philosophical and not get carried away.

There is nothing flashy about Taylor as he picks up his runs in a calm, unruffled manner, but at the same time he is always on the lookout for a chance to hit the loose ball to the boundary. He has the rare talent of being able to chisel out runs even when he is struggling to stay afloat.

Fittingly for a man who graduated as a surveyor from the University of NSW in 1987, his batting is solid and analytical with an eye for detail. Claiming that Taylor's broad backside looks like the omnibus edition of *Wisden's*, the *Australian's* Terry Brindle points out that he has the cocoon mentality possessed by the game's very best players. Brindle says: 'Taylor is efficient and effective and makes the game look simple without presuming to make it look easy. Einstein developed a theory of relativity on similar lines.'

Those who believe the bush is the lifeblood of Australian cricket were delighted by Taylor's incredible rise to be an automatic choice as an opener in any World XI. No one pampers you in the bush, but NSW country boys like Don Bradman, Bill O'Reilly, Stan McCabe, Alan Davidson and Doug Walters had the necessary get-up-and-go to claw their way to the top.

As his father was a valuator with the State Bank, Mark was born in Leeton on 27 October 1964 and spent his childhood in Mildura, Goulburn, West Wyalong and finally Wagga Wagga, where he first played competition cricket.

Taught the basics by his dad in the driveway of their Wagga home, Taylor recalls making 116 for Lake Albert in an Under-14 game in Wagga and being congratulated by Geoff Lawson, who played for the same club before reaching the lofty heights of the NSW team.

After playing for the Australian Under 19s with Steve and Mark Waugh and Craig McDermott against Sri Lanka, Taylor scored so many runs for the Northern District club in Sydney that he forced his way into the State side. Although he was a consistent run-getter from the start with 937 at 49.3 in his debut season in 1985–86, Taylor was a much slower scorer than he is now and was nicknamed Stodge.

Good moments and erratic times followed in the next season, so in a bid to improve his footwork and put more oomph into his drives and cuts, he went to Greenmount in the Bolton 50-over League in England as club professional. Taylor recalls: 'If you are the pro, everybody expects you to get runs each week and get them quickly. The pressure was on, but I loved it. My feet began to move three times quicker, so my cutting and driving became more assured and my confidence grew.'

Noting Taylor's more assured batting and sharp catching at first slip, Australian coach Bob Simpson beca .ie convinced the NSW player was the man for whom he had been searching.

Simpson was instrumental in splitting the already successful Test pairing of Geoff Marsh and David Boon to push Taylor into the opening spot. He explains:

> We wanted a left-hander at the top, but not just any left-hander. We waited until we felt we had the right one and Mark has turned out to be an enormous asset. I think he is the best slip we've had since Greg Chappell. He's enormously talented, with lovely hands and the ability to cover a lot of distance.

As basic as bricks and mortar, Taylor (219) and Marsh (138) quickly won a niche in the record books with a monumental opening stand of 329 against England in the fifth Test at Trent Bridge to dwarf Bob Simpson's and Bill Lawry's previous mark of 201. When Marsh finally lost his wicket on the second morning of play, Gower called for a glass of champagne at lunch to celebrate the breakthrough.

No player is immune to an early dismissal, but as with Lawry and Simpson, the batsmen who followed Taylor and Marsh usually get the chance to shower, sit down, relax and gather their thoughts for the task ahead. They know the Australian openers are blood and guts men with a hunger for runs.

Using a bat weighing 2lb 8oz, Taylor had begun the series with a magnificent opener's knock of 136 at Leeds, thus joining Charles Bannerman, Harry Graham, Bill Ponsford, Archie Jackson, Neil Harvey, Doug Walters, Greg Chappell and Kepler Wessels as the only players to score a century in their first Test innings against England.

The ball was swinging and cutting in a heavy atmosphere under a gloomy sky after England captain David Gower invited Australia to bat. By the time Allan Border's men had climbed to a first innings tally of 7 for 601, Gower's gamble was hailed by the English critics as an error of judgment only slightly less serious than the decision to send the Anzacs climbing the cliffs at Gallipoli.

Taylor had a couple of glasses of champagne when dining with his proud parents after finishing the first day with 96 runs against his name and paused to change his bat after beginning the second morning with a single. Then he clipped Derek Pringle off his hip to the fine leg boundary to bring up a century which drew an ovation from the crowd and his team-mates on the dressing room balcony.

Surely that must be the 100 Taylor cherishes above all others? Surprisingly it isn't, and Mark explains:

Even though it was my first Test 100 in my first game against England, I wouldn't put it ahead of the 101 I got against the Pakistanis in the Melbourne Test the following January. Everything at Leeds was in it for the batters. It was a really good wicket where we made 7 for 601 and they got 430 first up, and the outfield was lightning fast.

Fortunately I got through the hard times and went on and got that bogey 100 out of the way. It was good to get it, but I don't think I'd rate it as highly as the hundred against Pakistan.

With Wasim Akram, Waqar Younis, Imran Khan and Tauseef Ahmed, the Pakistanis had a good attack and the wicket had plenty in it for the bowlers. We made 223 and they got 107, so to make 52 in the first innings and 101 in the second on a bowler's wicket made it a pretty good match for me. Wasim Akram got 11 wickets, so to keep him out and make 100 in trying circumstances was really pleasing.

The difficult thing about Akram is that he can swing both the new and old ball both ways at a good pace. He lands it on the right spot, too. A lot of other bowlers in the world swing the ball a lot, but Akram swings it at a lively pace. I recall a couple of hooks against Younis which I hit really well in front of square leg. Shots I hadn't played for a while, but they just seemed to come.

Akram was fairly full in length, trying to get me to nick one. I played and missed quite a bit and had more than my fair share of luck. When they couldn't get me out there, they brought on Younis, who's got some good pace, and he tried to vary things by using the short ball a bit more than Akram.

I'd bracket Akram with Curtly Ambrose of the West Indies as the most difficult bowler I've faced. Towering over you from a height of 6ft 8in, Ambrose hits the bat higher up than the others. Right up in the splice, whereas Malcolm Marshall skids them through. The thing about the West Indies is that they have four blokes who bowl very quick and keep the pressure on all the time.

Putting Taylor's skills under the microscope, former Australian captain Ian Chappell says:

One of Mark's strengths is his approach. His technique is sound but simple. He accumulates runs at a rapid rate, but with an ease which often belies the quality of the opposition bowling. He has a good cricketing brain which has allowed him to improve rapidly and stay calm in all situations. He also knows where he is in relation to his off stump. He rarely plays at balls outside off stump unless he wants to thrash them through the covers or belt them off the back foot past point.

Forty minutes before the start of the 1989–90 Sheffield Shield final in Sydney, Taylor was told he was to lead NSW in their most significant encounter in ages after Geoff Lawson dropped out in the pre-match net warm-up with a shoulder injury.

Although he had never before led a team at first class level, Taylor accepted the appointment phlegmatically, lost the toss and batted all day for an unbeaten century. In fact, he sunk Queensland's hopes almost on his own with a double of 127 and 100. This confirmed suspicions that Taylor is indeed the man with the best credentials to take over the leadership baton from Allan Border when he eventually decides to pass it on.

Not surprisingly for a man who plays with such commonsense, Taylor shuns superstitions, although he admits:

> I had a few little things that I used to do, but I don't do them any more. It's your own ability and a bit of luck, not whether you're wearing a gold chain or putting on one pad before the other.
>
> I'm not a heavy practiser, although I enjoy practising. I don't like having a bat in my hand every day. It does me just as much good to get away for a couple of games of golf.

A likeable chap of integrity, warmth, wit and heart who is a single-figure marker at Pennant Hills club in Sydney, Taylor loves to escape with wife Judi to Halfway Creek near Coffs Harbour, where they golf and fish for snapper and gold-spotted sweetlips.

Mark was surprised that the Australian selectors broke up the successful Geoff Marsh–David Boon combination to give him a Test spot, and he remains grateful for the encouragement he got from the pair. Taylor comments:

> Geoff and David had being doing the business for quite a few years, but they were tremendous when I first came into the Australian side. Instead of making me feel as though I'd broken up a marriage, they made me so welcome. More than anyone else, in fact. David told me he was happy to bat at three.
>
> Deep down, I knew I had the shots and the ability to play Test cricket. I like being under pressure because it makes me concentrate all the time. Batting all day with Marshy to break the record at Trent Bridge was something special.

Greg Chappell says: 'I see a special quality in Mark Taylor. Richie Benaud, Sir Donald Bradman and Ian Chappell all had a hard, calculating edge to their character and it's obvious from the way Taylor bats that he has the steely heart necessary in a successful Australian captain.'

AUSTRALIA v PAKISTAN
Melbourne, 12–16 January 1990

Australia

	First innings		Second innings	
G.R. Marsh	c Yousuf b Akram	30	c Akram b Aaqib	24
M.A. Taylor	c Aaqib Imran	52	c Aamir b Tauseef	101
D.C. Boon	lbw b Akram	0	run out	21
A.R. Border	c Miandad b Akram	24	not out	62
D.M. Jones	c Yousuf b Imran	0	lbw b Akram	10
S.R. Waugh	c Yousuf b Aaqib	20	c Yousuf b Akram	3
P.R. Sleep	lbw b Akram	23	b Akram	0
I.R. Healey	c Shoaib b Aaqib	48	c Ijaz b Akram	25
M.C. Hughes	c Mansoor b Akram	8	c Mansoor b Akram	32
T.M.Alderman	c Aamir b Sakram	0	not out	1
C.G. Rackemann	not out	0		
Sundries		18		33
		223		8 (dec) for 312

	O	M	R	W	O	M	R	W
Imran Khan	18	6	53	2	8	2	21	0
Wasim Akram	30	9	62	6	41.4	12	98	5
Aaqib Javed	22.1	7	47	2	21	2	55	1
Waqar Younis	12	3	27	0	22	4	68	0
Tauseef Ahmed	8	1	25	0	16	3	58	1

Fall of wickets
First innings: 90, 90, 98, 98, 131, 148, 201, 223, 223, 223
Second innings: 73, 116, 204, 216, 220, 260, 305

Pakistan

	First innings		Second innings	
Aamir Malik	lbw b Alderman	7	c Taylor b Hughes	0
Shoaib Mohammad	c Healey b Alderman	6	c Boon b Hughes	10
Mansoor Akhtar	c Taylor b Rackemann	5	lbw b Alderman	14
Javed Miandad	c Healey b Alderman	3	lbw b Waugh	65
Ijaz Ahmed	c Taylor b Hughes	19	c Marsh b Hughes	121
Imran Khan	c Alderman b Rackemann	3	lbw b Alderman	45
Salim Yousuf	c Taylor b Hughes	16	lbw b Alderman	38
Wasim Akram	c Healey b Hughes	6	c Taylor b Sleep	6
Tauseef Ahmed	not out	9	not out	14
Waqar Younis	lbw b Sleep	18	lbw b Alderman	4
Aaqib Javed	c Healey b Rackemann	0	lbw b Alderman	0
Sundries		15		19
		107		336

	O	M	R	W	O	M	R	W
Alderman	19	6	30	3	33.5	6	105	5
Rackemann	21.5	8	32	3	38	13	67	0
Hughes	17	7	34	3	42	14	79	3
Sleep	8	5	6	1	21	7	64	1
Waugh					3	0	13	1

Fall of wickets
First innings: 12, 20, 20, 44, 44, 65, 71, 71, 106, 107
Second innings: 4, 23, 31, 134, 218, 291, 303, 328, 333, 336

Australia won by 92 runs

HIGHEST SCORES BY AUSTRALIANS IN FIRST CLASS CRICKET

SCORE	BATSMAN	MATCH	VENUE	SEASON
452*	Don Bradman	NSW *v.* Qld	*Sydney*	1929–30
437	Bill Ponsford	Vic. *v.* Qld	*Melbourne*	1927–28
429	Bill Ponsford	Vic. *v.* Tas.	*Melbourne*	1922–23
383	Charles Gregory	NSW *v.* Qld	*Brisbane*	1906–07
369	Don Bradman	SA *v.* Tas.	*Adelaide*	1935–36
365	Clem Hill	SA *v.* NSW	*Adelaide*	1900–01
359	Bob Simpson	NSW *v.* Qld	*Brisbane*	1963–64
357	Don Bradman	SA *v.* Vic.	*Melbourne*	1935–36
355*	Geoff Marsh	WA *v.* SA	*Perth*	1989–90
352	Bill Ponsford	Vic. *v.* NSW	*Melbourne*	1926–27
345	Charlie Macartney	Aust. *v.* Notts	*Nottingham*	1921
340*	Don Bradman	NSW *v.* Vic.	*Sydney*	1928–29
336	Bill Ponsford	Vic. *v.* SA	*Melbourne*	1927–28
334	Don Bradman	Aust. *v.* Eng.	*Leeds*	1930
325*	Hunter Hendry	Vic. *v.* NZ	*Melbourne*	1925–26
325	Charlie Badcock	SA *v.* Vic.	*Adelaide*	1935–36
321	William Murdoch	NSW *v.* Vic.	*Sydney*	1881–82
315*	Alan Kippax	NSW *v.* Qld	*Sydney*	1927–28
311	Bob Simpson	Aust. *v.* Eng.	*Manchester*	1964
307	Bob Cowper	Aust. *v.* Eng.	*Melbourne*	1965–66
306*	David Hookes	SA *v.* Tas.	*Adelaide*	1986–87
304	Don Bradman	Aust. *v.* Eng.	*Leeds*	1934
303*	Warwick Armstrong	Aust. *v.* Somerset	*Bath*	1905
300*	Victor Trumper	Aust. *v.* Sussex	*Hove*	1899

* Not out.

RECORD TEST PARTNERSHIPS BY AUSTRALIANS

WKT	SCORE	BATSMAN	OPP. TEAM	VENUE	SEASON
1st	383	Bill Lawry and Bob Simpson	*v.* WI	*Bridgetown*	1964–65
2nd	451	Bill Ponsford and Don Bradman	*v.* Eng.	*The Oval*	1934
3rd	295	Colin McDonald and Neil Harvey	*v.* WI	*Kingston*	1954–55
4th	388	Bill Ponsford and Don Bradman	*v.* Eng.	*Leeds*	1934
5th	405	Sid Barnes and Don Bradman	*v.* Eng.	*Sydney*	1946–47
6th	346	Jack Fingleton and Don Bradman	*v.* Eng.	*Melbourne*	1936–37
7th	217	Doug Walters and Gary Gilmour	*v.* NZ	*Christchurch*	1976–77
8th	243	Clem Hill and Roger Hartigan	*v.* Eng.	*Adelaide*	1907–08
9th	154	Syd Gregory and Jack Blackham	*v.* Eng.	*Sydney*	1894–95
10th	127	Johnny Taylor and Arthur Mailey	*v.* Eng.	*Sydney*	1924–25

INDEX

Y